Sailing with Scoundrels and Kings

A Lifetime of Boating

John Jourdane

CAPE HORN PRESS
SEAL BEACH, CALIFORNIA

This book is dedicated to the Sea,
and all the men and women who sail upon it.

To Scott,

Best wishes,

John Jordan

Acknowledgements

A special thank you to Geri Conser for the cover photo, John Balzar and the *Los Angeles Times* for use of John's Ragtime article, and John Rousmanierre for use of his article on the Bermuda Race.

Thank you to Scott Stocking and Dana Cole at RJ Communications Editorial Service for a great job editing my scribbling and wayward thoughts. And to Jonathan Gullery at Budget Book Design for making the book design and cover come together beautifully.

Thank you Rich Roberts, Rob Moore, Herb McCormick, Kimball Livingston, Chuck Hawley, Brad Avery, and Kitty James for your support.

And a special thanks to the "Kings," who have allowed me to sail on their boats over the years: Roy Disney, Sumner "Huey" Long, Hasso Platner, Pat Farrah, Bob Lane, Larry Harvey, Digby Taylor, Grant Dalton, John DeLaura, Doug Baker, Peter Tong, Art and Libbie Kamisugi, Rodney Inaba, George Bodley, Dr. Jim Ward, Dr. Ted Burns, Dr. Paul McCullough, Bob and Nancy Gosnell, Mike Keeler, Dr. Neil Barth, Scott Zimmerman, Don Clothier, Sandy Horowitz, Manouch Moshayedi, Milt Vogel, James McDowell, Greg Au, Joe Case, Rick Shema, and Rex and Clarie Kosack.

Contents

Prologue

I was twelve and my brother, Mo, was fourteen. We were visiting our sister, Barbara, in Long Beach, California. Our days were filled with swimming in Alamitos Bay, riding our bikes along the shoreline, and chasing the elusive "grunion" as they came ashore to lay their eggs in the soft sand of Long Beach. We would lie on the sand on our beach towels for hours watching the small sailboats fly up and down the Bay in the warm sea breeze.

One day, while riding our bikes on the Peninsula, we saw a small shack on an old wooden pier with a sign saying "Boat Rentals." We stopped to investigate and found that we could rent a little sailboat for the princely sum of $5.00 for the day. We talked it over that night and decided to pool our money and rent one the next day. It looked like great fun, and it couldn't be that hard to sail. So, the next day we rode our bikes to Bay Boat Rentals and said we would like to rent a sailboat. The owner, looked at us and said, "Do you know how to sail?" Mo and I looked at each other and then said, "Yes." Actually neither of us had set foot in a boat before, but we didn't want to lose our big chance to go sailing. The owner said he had an old Naples Sabot he would rent us for $5.00 plus a $20.00 deposit. The $5.00 was okay, but the deposit was a problem. He reluctantly let us leave our bicycles as a deposit and took us out to the boat.

It was an old Sabot that needed paint and a fresh coat of varnish, but it looked like a yacht to us. "She's yours for the afternoon. Rig her up and go have fun," the owner said as we looked at a bare hull, a mast, a sail, a rudder, a leeboard, and a bunch of rope. We had no clue how to put it all together and make a functioning sailboat. As we pondered the problem, a young girl sailed in with her boat fully rigged, and we started assembling our boat to look like hers. We had trouble figuring out how the rudder attached to the back of the boat, but eventually we got it all together, and climbed in.

We had to play around with the tiller and let the rope attached to the sail go in and out to get the boat moving, but we eventually did. We took off down the bay. What great fun! We were sailing—just flying across the water having a grand time!

We had one problem. We were sailing downwind, and there was a low bridge coming up at the end of the bay. I turned the tiller to sail the other way—back up the bay—and the boat headed into the wind and stopped. It wouldn't turn either way. It was stuck heading straight into the wind. I had my first experience with "being in irons." Maybe this sailing wasn't so easy after all. No one had told us about tacking.

Mo and I solved the problem by jumping out of the boat and swimming it the beach. We towed it back up to the top of the bay, hopped in, and happily sailed down the bay again until we hit the bridge, hopped out, swam the boat ashore, and walked it up the bay. Thus we spent our first day of yachting.

I knew there must be an easier way to do it. The other kids weren't hopping out of their boats every time they got to the bridge. They just turned around and went sailing back into the wind. This was perplexing. Every time I tried it, the boat headed straight into the wind and stopped. In the following days, I wandered along the bay, watching the boats as they went back and forth, and I started to get an idea of tacking. I met a boy my age named George, who was taking a class from the Parks and Recreation Department. He said I should sign up. I did, and I finally learned how to rig a boat and how to tack. I found this was much easier than jumping out and swimming the boat to shore.

That was the beginning of a 45-year journey on which I would sail over 300,000 miles, cross the Pacific Ocean 47 times, cross the Atlantic Ocean 12 times, and sail around the world 3 times—including twice in the Whitbread Round the World Race (now known as the Volvo Round the World Race). Every voyage has been different, and I have never stopped learning.

The Navy has a slogan similar to: "Become a Sailor, and See the World!" I did become a sailor, and I have seen the world, but more important than all the places I've seen, are all the wonderful, interesting, and strange people I've met along the way. And that is what this book is about: the people—the scoundrels and the kings.

Feel free to consult the glossary at the end of the book.

One

Hawaii

I graduated from UCLA with a degree in zoology and then spent two years in Colombia, teaching biology in the Peace Corps. I returned to California, where I taught migrant farm worker children in the San Jaoquin Valley and earned a master's degree in education at USC. Then I moved to Hawaii and taught science at the Kamehameha Schools in Honolulu. Living in Hawaii would play a huge roll in my sailing future.

While teaching at Kamehameha, I met Vern Bixby, who was a biology teacher at the high school and had a twenty-five-foot sailboat, which he kept at and raced out of Kaneohe Bay. Vern always needed a crew, and, when he found out I could sail, he immediately took me in as a regular crewman.

We raced the little sloop in all the local races on the bay and up and down the windward side of Oahu. Sailing in the Hawaiian trade winds was eye-opening for me. I had learned to sail in the calm waters off Southern California where small craft warnings are raised if the wind gets above twenty knots. In Hawaii the winds rarely get below twenty knots, and the swells are usually ten to fifteen feet high.

In 1972 I bought my own boat, a Columbia 26 sloop, and named it *Kuhela*. I had a great time on it. On weekends I would sail with some friends or by myself upwind to Molokai, Lanai, or Maui. The channel crossings could be quite rough. After a hard day of sailing, we would

Kuhela moored at Captain Cook, Hawaii

anchor in a protected bay, barbeque fish we had caught, drink a couple beers, then sleep like logs on the gently rocking deck. At first light, we would have a cup of coffee, raise the anchor and sails, and head downwind back to Oahu, arriving as the sun was setting. It was a fun, relaxing time of my life. I had no family to deal with, I was young, healthy, and strong, and I had a boat I could sail on whenever I wanted.

One spring break, I sailed with Calvin Ho, a fellow teacher at Kamehameha, to the north shore of Molokai. Cal had just returned from a stint in the Peace Corps in Palau, Micronesia, and was a true Polynesian. We anchored in Pelekunu Bay. It was a valley that was totally isolated from the rest of Molokai by steep cliffs and a rough rocky shoreline. At one time it was inhabited by Hawaiians, but it is now a deserted, tropical paradise. Cal made our chopsticks and plates from palm fronds. We dove for slipper lobster in the bay and freshwater prawns in the stream. We plucked 'Opihi shells from the rocks and ate them raw. We found wild guava, passion fruit, and coconuts. We even made our own poi from wild taro plants. We took showers in a waterfall and slept in the open under warm, starry Hawaiian skies. It was a week I would later reflect on while sailing in a blizzard on the Great Lakes and in the freezing Southern Ocean in the Whitbread Round the World Race.

Back in Honolulu, I met Art and Libbie Kamisugi. They owned an Ericson 39 called *Libalia*, named after Libbie and their daughter Malia. We raced and sailed *Libalia* to all the Hawaiian Islands and in most of the local races. Some of my best years of sailing happened on *Libalia* with Art, Libbie, George Norcross, and Dave Soderland. The boat was designed to the International Offshore Racing rule, with round topsides and a lot of sail area. It wasn't the best design for the big winds and seas around Hawaii; we spent many downwind runs rocking wildly side to side and wiping out in broaches, both regular and "Chinese jibes (the boat rounding down instead of rounding up)." But we also had wonderful times on the *Libalia* sailing to all the islands and spending weekends anchored in little coves on Kauai, Maui, Lanai, as well as sailing along the north shore of Molokai. Art is an avid fisherman and had rigged *Libalia* up with serious fishing gear. We would go fishing for big game fish like marlin and tuna. Art knew where to fish; he always seemed to come home with fish.

We would often sail the boat to Lanai, anchor for the night, and then go over to Lahaina, Maui. We would spend another night there, having a few drinks at the Lahaina Inn. Then we would sail back to Oahu by the north shore of Molokai, where Art would seem to always catch big fish.

Overleaf: Libalia racing off Diamond Head with spinnaker and blooper.

Libalia

On one three-day weekend, we sailed the boat to Niihau to go fishing off Kaula Rock. We anchored off Niihau, then sailed the boat to Hanalei Bay on Kauai. The crew got off and flew back to Honolulu to go to work, and I was to sail the boat back with a friend flying in from Honolulu. Well, my friend called on the radio and said he couldn't make it. So I was stuck with sailing the boat back by myself (an eighteen-hour beat across the Kauai Channel), or trying to find some crew on Kauai to help me deliver the boat. I was in the local market getting some provisions, so I put a notice on the bulletin board and rowed the dinghy back to the boat at anchor in the bay. I was checking the engine when there was a knock on the hull. I went on deck to find a bearded young man in the water holding on the anchor line. He said his name was Dennis, and he had seen my note in the store. He and his girlfriend Pam would like to help me sail the boat back to Honolulu. I invited him aboard and inquired if they knew how to sail, and he said yes, they had both done a lot of sailing. I told Dennis to bring Pam and be ready on the beach at 9 AM. Then I asked if they were prone to seasickness, because I had Dramamine and Bonine if they needed it. He said no, they were "pure." They had been living in a tree house down the beach and had been fasting for weeks.

Dennis and Pam were on the beach in the morning, and we rowed out to *Libalia*. I hoisted the anchor, raised the mainsail, and we motored out of Hanalei Bay. As soon as we reached open water, both Dennis and Pam started throwing up. They proceeded to take off all their clothes and went below (they were used to being "pure"). I set the jib and started sailing toward Oahu. About every half hour, Dennis would come on deck, go to the rail, and throw up, then look around and say, "This is far out, man," then go back below to lie down with Pam. This went on for the next eighteen hours. Luckily, I was able to tighten the brake on the wheel, and go below to make coffee, a sandwich, or do some navigation.

I steered, trimmed sails, and navigated the boat to Waikiki single-handed. Dennis and Pam finally came on deck as we were motoring into the Ala Wai Boat Harbor. They said they had a great sail, and as they walked off the boat, Dennis handed me a plastic bag. I said goodbye and thanked them for "all the help." I looked at the bag and found it was full of hashish! I walked to the nearest dumpster and threw it in. Yes, Dennis and Pam were really "pure."

Carrie Ann V

Owner: Rodney Inaba
Crew: Sonny Nelson, Larry Stenek, John Bingham,
John Jourdane, Joe Dolan, Pat Kudlik, Joe Dolan, Tom Wilson.

In 1978, I hooked up with the crew of *Carrie Ann V*, a Bruce Farr-designed 36-footer that was doing a lot of racing in Hawaii and winning. The owner, Rodney, decided to race in the 1978 Pan Am Clipper Cup. This was a very serious team. We practiced every Tuesday night and raced every Friday night in the beer can race out of Hawaii Yacht Club and then raced the weekend races around Oahu or to the other islands. *Carrie Ann V* needed a navigator for the Clipper Cup series, and Rodney asked me if I would come along and race with them. It was a serious racing team, with many hours of practice, and the practice paid off. We ended up winning our class in the Clipper Cup.

The Around the State Race was a 700-miler. The race instructions just said, "Leave all the islands to port." It was a long, hard race, taking almost 5 days to complete. We left Waikiki, sailed down the windward side of Oahu, across the Kauai Channel to the island of Kauai, then around the island of Niihau, and then a 350-mile reach to South Cape on the island of Hawaii. We then beat up the windward shore of Hawaii, then set spin-nakers and ran along the windward shores of Maui and Molokai, across the Molokai Channel to the finish line at Diamond Head on Oahu. It was a very long race on a 36-foot stripped-out racing machine. But it was a lot of fun, and I made friends who are still my friends today.

Our major competition for the Clipper Cup was a Farr 36 from New Zealand called *Country Boy*. We sailed close to each other for the whole series, and drank a lot of beers together after each race. I became close friends with Lin Carmichael, whom I would run into again in the next Clipper Cup two years later.

Two

Aquarius —
Honolulu to Tahiti

While working in the boatyard in Honolulu, I met George Bodley, who owned a Cheoy Lee Offshore 36 sloop named *Aquarius*. I got to know George well and spent many evenings over a beer at the Hawaii Yacht Club talking about our boats and sailing the South Seas. George had decided to sail his boat from Hawaii to Tahiti with his girlfriend and needed crew. I talked it over with my girlfriend, Muffet, and we decided to go. The real reason George invited me was that I had a sextant and supposedly knew how to use it. This was in the years before GPS or even Loran. I had taken a class in celestial navigation but had never really used it at sea.

We went through *Aquarius* from top to bottom, checking all the gear, mast, and rigging. We bought provisions for a month at sea and found places for it all on the boat. We loaded on fuel and water, and left Ala Wai Boat Harbor, on a clear starry night for Tahiti.

The Molokai Channel was quite rough as we crossed from Honolulu to the island of Molokai, but the boat seemed to handle it well. We tacked up the north shore of Molokai, and the winds kept freshening and pushing us toward the high cliffs of the island. The winds were quite strong, blowing twenty to twenty-five knots, with twelve- to eighteen-foot seas. It was not very pleasurable sailing.

Aquarius and crew ready to leave the Ala Wai Yacht Harbor

As we sailed past the north shore of Maui near Haleakala, the wind and seas abated, but then built up again in the Alenuihaha Channel between Maui and the Island of Hawaii. It was still blowing pretty hard, so we decided to stop at Hilo to dry out the boat and get ice and fuel. Everything on board was wet! We anchored in a beautiful little cove called Reed's Bay next to the Orchid Isle Hotel.

The next morning we motored into Radio Bay to get water, but it was too crowded. Instead, we went to the commercial fishing pier in Hilo Harbor and pulled every thing in the boat on deck in the sun to let it dry out. A friendly Hawaiian guy named Kimo came by and asked us if we needed any help. He took us in his truck to get ice, and the iceman gave us a big bag of cucumbers he had grown in his garden.

We powered back to Reed's Bay, and went shopping for last minute provisions at the Hilo Mall. We took showers on the beach, straightened up the boat, and then left our mooring as the sun went down.

Once we got away from the Islands, the wind and seas calmed down and were more organized. We were close reaching* in fifteen knots of wind and getting lots of easting. As my navigation teacher, Louis Vallier, said: "Easting in the Pacific is like money in the bank."

I broke out the sextant, and managed to get a decent sun sight. We had made 152 miles, noon to noon. The wind and seas had built back up a bit, but the sailing was pleasurable. We put out the fishing line for the first time and were visited by a pod of porpoise. In Hawaii, porpoise and rainbows are signs of good luck.

The weather was beautiful, sunny, and clear. We took saltwater showers on the stern of the boat and put out a second fishing line. We had traveled 176 miles in our second twenty-four-hour run. We had a nice steak dinner. A flying fish landed on deck and we were going to keep it for breakfast, but we felt sorry for it, so we let it go. George found another flying fish on deck, and ate it raw, right on the spot.

We were comfortably sailing along, when the boat suddenly headed into the wind. It wouldn't respond to the steering wheel. Something had broken in the steering system. I dove overboard to check the rudder, and it looked fine. It turned out to be the steering cable, so we hooked up the emergency tiller while we fixed the cable. We caught two small fish that look like mackerel, and had a 1000-mile-out cocktail party with drinks, peanuts, and sashimi. We opened our 1000-mile-out presents, which were books to read, clean T-shirts, and bottles of booze.

The next morning we woke up to a broken self-steering vane and George's announcement that he had diarrhea. Not a great day! There were big, dark clouds ahead, and it rained all day. We managed to fix the steering vane and George's diarrhea.

When the rain squalls passed, and the sun came out, all was fine with the world. We were reaching along and enjoying the calm seas when a dark brown bird came to visit. I thought it was a stormy petrel. I started taking sun sights with my sextant every two hours in the hope of pinpointing our position.

It was a sunny, calm day. We were all relaxing on deck and reading, when a huge rain squall came through. It really poured, so we filled all our buckets with fresh water and took showers in the rain. We were all squeaky clean as we passed the half-way point to Tahiti.

It was a rainy and windy night. We lost one of the fishing lures during the night, probably taken by a shark. We had arrived in the Doldrums, and the weather was very changeable, with little wind and lots of rain squalls. We would sail ahead of the squalls in a lot of wind, and then motor through the calm after they went through.

The next day was beautiful, calm, and sunny. We took showers, read, and George baked fresh cookies. I finally got a perfect three-star fix with the sextant, and decided that by the time we reached Tahiti, I would probably have figured out the sextant.

The winds picked up from the southeast. We were in the southeast trades! We crossed the equator and were visited by King Neptune (George in costume). We had a big equator-crossing party with cocktails, streamers, and a great ham dinner.

The boat was heeling over, and we had to move around at an angle. We had beautiful seagoing plates that stick well to the table on an angle, but the food slid off the plates onto the cabin sole, so we started eating all meals from bowls. We had about 700 miles to go to Tahiti. We caught a nice mahimahi and fried it up for dinner. It was delicious!

The wind and seas died down and the sun came out. We all sunbathed and showered, then discussed our approach to Tahiti. We decided to stop at Tikehau, a small atoll in the Tuamotu Island chain, which was right in our path to Papeete, the capital of Tahiti.

The good weather stayed with us, and we close reached in fifteen knots of wind and small seas. The seas were calm enough that I even cooked pancakes, even though we had lost our spatula.

Our "family" on the island of Mataiva

We caught another mahimahi and had it for lunch. Mahimahi are incredibly beautiful as they come aboard after being caught. They go through wild changes in color as they die; from green to brilliant gold to gray.

The wind died, so we powered all night with no wind. The morning brought big rain squalls, so we all took freshwater showers. The crew was getting anxious about landfall. We had not seen land in over two weeks, and everyone was wondering if I really knew what I was doing with that sextant.

I told them, we should see Tikehau the next morning, but there are a lot of currents running through the Tuamotu Islands. A big squall came through with lots of wind, rain, and rough seas. We reefed the main, and changed to a smaller jib. The boat pounded all night, but it calmed down in the morning. When I took my morning sun sights, it looked like we were going to miss Tikehau. We didn't get far enough east. Old Louis Vallier was right.

Land Ho! At about 12 noon, we saw an island, which turned out to be Mataiva. As we motored close to the island, a local man dressed in a pareu waved for us to come in. He came out in a small boat and showed us a narrow passage, which we entered slowly. His name was Aroma. We threw out an anchor and tied mooring lines to coconut trees.

We went ashore, and were treated like royalty. The people in the little village gave us coconuts and shell leis and some beautiful shells. We gave them our eggs and chewing gum. What a beautiful serene island it was. We met Tauira, who was the village chief. Communication was difficult, as no one on the island spoke English, and only a few men spoke a little French. The local language is Tahitian.

We spent a couple of the most enjoyable days of our lives on Mataiva. It's hard to put into words the beauty, love, and aloha we experienced. We were picked up early in the morning and taken from our boat to a sumptuous breakfast of fresh homemade bread, cheese, and canned corned beef. We gave our hosts presents of canned food, fishing gear, mosquito coils, and candy. George and I went off with Aroma to see his house and caught a couple chickens for lunch. I played guitar and sang, and then our hosts sang.

We toured the island on motor scooters. It was a real "Mister Toad's Wild Ride." We visited two shipwrecks, a Spanish trader, and an old Tahiti ketch. We saw land crabs eating coconuts, and literally thousands of coconut trees. I went out on the reef with Torii, Tauira's son, and Muffet stayed in the village with the family. Torii adopted me as his special friend and made me sit by him wherever we went. We brought all our bottles of booze off the boat and gave them to our hosts. Then they said we had to have drinks, so they mixed everything altogether and we drank it. What a combination! They mixed gin, vodka, cognac, tequila, Kahlúa, crème de menthe, 7-Up, and Dr Pepper, into a big punch.

We had a feast for lunch with our family and the local magistrate-pastor. Rita, a boy, took us on a tour of the village. George and I played basketball with some in the local boys, and naturally, the locals won. We returned to the house for dinner. It was lovely, with the whole village singing songs and dancing for us. They really got a kick out of George and me trying to dance Tahitian-style. We started to leave, but there was too much rain so we sang and danced some more. We had two guests sleeping on board that night, Rita and Jean Louis. It was truly a day to remember.

All our new "family" came out in boats to help us leave, including the old Tutu (grandma). We invited them all aboard for breakfast (for ten), then gave them each gifts. Leaving was sad. I think we experienced true "aloha" as it was in the old days. We drifted slowly away from the island, waving good bye, knowing we had just experienced something very special. Once Mataiva was out of sight, we straightened up the boat, and got ready for our reentrance to "civilization." Next stop Tahiti.

We made landfall at six in the morning with Tahiti and Moorea in sight. They are really beautiful, just like Bali Hai in the movie *South Pacific*. We arrived in Papeete, and tied up "Tahiti-style" to the main quay and went to the customs office.

Our Mataiva family says goodbye, even old Tutu.

Barefoot in San Diego

Three

Barefoot—
San Diego to Seattle

In June 1976, I received a phone call from Jim Ward, a dentist in Bremerton, Washington, asking me if I could help him sail his new Cal 3-30, *Barefoot*, from San Diego to Seattle.

It turned out to be quite an adventure. The 900-mile trip took thirty days, and I stopped at almost every harbor between Mexico and Canada.

I flew to San Diego, and found Jim and *Barefoot* at the Half Moon Anchorage on Shelter Island. There was a long list of work to be done on the boat before we could leave. Jim and I put in a depth sounder, wired the instruments, and worked on the boat all day. I met the rest of the crew, Clark and Gretchen, who lived on their own boat in San Diego.

We worked on the boat all the next day, went shopping for various gear and provisions, then cast off from Half Moon Anchorage about midnight—destination: Santa Catalina Island.

We motored all night with no wind. In the morning, after the sun came out, the wind slowly filled, and it was a beautiful day of sailing. We sailed in close to Avalon but decided to continue on to the isthmus at the west end of the Island. We tied up to a mooring in Fourth of July Cove, and Jim made a very delicious casserole for dinner.

We left early in the morning for Santa Barbara, and had a beautiful day of sailing in the light air and flat seats. I practiced taking fixes with a hand bearing compass, and got five LOPs (lines of Position) on the islands, a perfect no triangle fix. We crossed shipping lanes and saw several large ships going both north and south.

We arrived at Santa Barbara Harbor early in the morning in a light rain. It was a little scary going in, because of the shoaling near the breakwater, plus it was very hard to see in the misty early morning light. But we arrived safely and were given a nice slip from the harbormaster. We spent the day shopping and sightseeing in Santa Barbara. It's a really pretty little town with a quaint mall zigzagging down State Street. We found a great fruit and nut store where we loaded up for the voyage. We left early in the morning for Morro Bay. If it were too rough to round Point Conception, "Cape Horn of the Pacific," we would seek protected anchorage in Cojo.

Point Conception was fairly calm, so we decided to continue on to Morro Bay. But once we passed Point Arguello it started to get windy and the seas built up. By the time we reached Point Sal, it was blowing thirty-five knots and gusting to forty. Jim was very sick, so we decided we should put into Port San Luis instead of Morro Bay. It was just too rough. I tied up to the fuel dock and Gretchen called the local hospital about Jim. We put him in a taxi with Gretchen, and sent them to the hospital. Gretchen left Jim at the hospital, came back, and we went to dinner at a restaurant on the pier. After dinner, we moved the boat out to a mooring. We were worried about Jim.

The next morning I called the hospital to find out about Jim. The medical staff thought it was either flu or exhaustion. We were stuck in Port San Luis and just had to wait. But it was a nice place to be stuck.

We met the members of the San Luis Yacht Club, and they were incredibly friendly. One member let us borrow a dinghy to get back and forth from the mooring, and others offered their homes for us to take showers.

I called Jim at the hospital, and after talking it over, we decided I should take the boat up to Morro Bay, where they had better facilities. So we left Port San Luis, and sailed around Point Buchon and into Morro Bay, where we tied up at the Morro Bay Yacht Club. There were five other boats there. They had turned back after trying to head north, but found it too rough as they approached Point Sur.

We had to move the boat out to a mooring while the club had their Sunday races. They had some strange boats racing, many of them home-made, including a canoe with two El Toro dinghy sails, and two lasers lashed together as a catamaran. I called Jim at the hospital in San Luis Obispo, and he sounded awful. It turned out he had pneumonia. He said that I should take the boat up to San Francisco as soon as the wind died down.

We filled the water tanks, cleaned the boat, did some shopping, and left Morro Bay in the afternoon. We planned to sail north to San Simeon, where there is a nice anchorage under the hills where the Hearst Castle is located. The weather was really calm, so we kept motoring on to Monterey. The coastline of Big Sur was absolutely beautiful.

We ran out of fuel off Carmel and had to pour some in the tank from jerry cans. We had to prime the engine to get it started. We arrived at Monterey Harbor in the evening and were given yet another nice slip from the harbormaster. Monterey seemed very busy after the quiet beauty of Big Sur.

We left to Monterey in the morning to sail to Santa Cruz. It was fun sailing across Monterey Bay in strong winds, reaching along at good speed. We arrived around 1500 hours and got a slip from the harbormaster. My brother, Mo, and his friend David Steingass were waiting for us at the dock, so I brought them aboard and showed them the boat. I left Clark and Gretchen with the boat, and I went with Mo to his house in Aptos to have a shower and dinner.

We left Santa Cruz and sailed north towards Half Moon Bay, with a new crewmember, my brother, Tom Jourdane. The wind was very light, so we motor-sailed on calm seas. We stopped in Half Moon Bay to get fuel, then continued north.

The trip to San Francisco was uneventful. We passed under the Golden Gate Bridge in the morning and motored into Sausalito. We found no slips available, so we tied up at the fuel dock for the night.

The next morning, we sailed across the bay to the San Francisco Small Boat Harbor and found a slip. There weren't any shower facilities, so I went to the St. Francis Yacht Club, and used my Hawaii Yacht Club card to get a courtesy card. St. Francis Yacht Club is a great facility. They treat their guests wonderfully, and they have a great bar and very nice showers.

Clark and Gretchen left to go back to San Diego because Jim had decided to put the boat on a truck to Seattle. Tom was a great help. We spent the morning waxing the topsides, and then he had to leave for Santa Cruz.

I watched the Fireball North American Championships off the St. Francis Yacht Club and then talked to Jim on the phone. He changed his mind and wanted me to continue taking the boat north. I had to find some crew to help me sail the boat from San Francisco to Washington.

I called my brothers, Mo and Tom. Mo decided to come along, but Tom couldn't, he had to work. Then I met Sandi Pensinger, a crewmember off the boat *Simply Super*. Her boat was stuck in San Francisco with engine problems, and she wanted to sail north with us. Sandi seemed like a very nice person and a competent sailor.

Steve Bergren, a friend from my Peace Corps days in Colombia, came by for a visit. I tried to recruit him to help me sail the boat north, but he couldn't get free from work.

I finally found the fourth crewman, Fred Forshay. He was inquiring about sailing on *Simply Super*, and Jilly, the owner of *Simply Super*, sent him over to me. He was a rigger from Newport Beach and seemed to know what he was doing.

We left San Francisco about 8 PM as the wind was calming down. But after we passed underneath the Golden Gate Bridge, it picked up and the seas started getting very confused. They call the area outside the Golden Gate "The Potato Patch" because it is so rough. It blew hard all night, with big breaking waves.

Once we rounded Point Reyes, the wind and seas died down, and it was a very nice sail to Bodega Bay. Mo called home and found out he had to leave. He worked for Governor Jerry Brown, and he was needed in Sacramento.

So, we left Bodega Bay with a crew of three—Sandi, Fred, and I—bound for Fort Bragg. The wind came up about 9 AM, and blew twenty-five knots all day. We had to tack up the coast into heavy wind and short, steep seas. We couldn't make much headway. It was a long, rough day, and it was starting to get dark, so we put into Havens Anchorage, which turned out to be a beautiful, little cove. We were very tired and chilled to the bone.

After a hot meal and a good night's sleep, we left for Fort Bragg early in the morning. The weather was the exact opposite of the day before, warm temperatures and a glassy calm ocean. We powered all day, and trolled a fishing line to try and catch a salmon. A lot of fishing boats were out, so we figured salmon must be around.

We arrived at Fort Bragg at about 3:30 PM, and went into the Noyo River to the boat basin. This was a real fishing town. Hundreds of fishing boats were tied up in the basin. We were the only sailboat there, and they didn't know what to make of us.

There were no slips available, so we rafted up to some small fishing boats. I bought a nice salmon from the boat we were tied to, and we had a great salmon dinner. I asked the skipper of the fishing boat, what was the key to catching salmon, and he gave me a special fishing lure.

We left Noyo River at about 5:00 AM, and we had to get in a parade of fishing boats heading out to the fishing grounds. There was no wind, and the seas were calm. We saw eight different sharks as we cruised up the coast. We put out our new fishing gear, and trolled for salmon all day with no luck. We arrived at Shelter Cove around 3:00 PM, had dinner, and then left about 10:00 PM for Eureka.

The area from Cape Mendocino to Eureka was very foggy in the morning. Maneuvering was very difficult because of the number of fishing boats out. We had to weave our way through them in the fog without radar. The salmon were running, and everyone who could find a boat was out fishing. We tied up at the Humboldt Yacht Club and spent the afternoon cleaning the boat with fresh water. We were a big event there, because Eureka didn't have many sailboats on the one hand, and on the other hand, they rarely had anyone come all away from San Diego. We met a nice couple on a fishing boat and had drinks with them in the afternoon. Henry, the skipper, gave us a salmon rig that he guaranteed would help us catch salmon. We watched Fourth of July fireworks across the Bay from their boat. It was a pleasant evening.

We left Eureka at about 6:00 AM in heavy fog and followed the parade of fishing boats out of the bay. It slowly cleared up and the sun finally came out by the afternoon. We ran out of fuel near Trinidad Head, so we went into the cove get some. It was a very strange harbor; quite small, filled with high rocks, but there were a couple hundred fishing boats moored there. We couldn't get into the gas dock, so we hailed a fisherman in a dinghy, and Fred jumped in with a jerry can and got five gallons of diesel, then came back out to *Barefoot* in the dinghy.

It was sunny and calm all afternoon with lots of sharks. We arrived at Crescent City in the dark. There was a beautiful new marina there. The harbormaster came down, welcomed us, and shook our hands. What a pleasant change from some of the harbors we had been in!

We spent the day at Crescent City cleaning the boat, shopping, and doing laundry. It was a peaceful, quaint town; not a fishing town or lumber town, but a country town. We saw a lot of farmers and pickup trucks. I didn't feel like I was in a sea port at all. Crescent City experienced a tsunami in 1964, and the whole town was rebuilt. It's very modern, but they kept its charm.

We left Crescent city at 6:00 AM. We decided to go through St. George Channel instead of outside the reef. It was calm and clear, and then the wind clocked to the South! I couldn't believe it. We actually had the wind behind us, not on the nose. We put up the big jib, and went wing and wing with the spinnaker pole holding the jib out. It was great sailing, and we were moving along at seven to eight knots. We jibed, and the wind picked up, and then we were surfing on the seas at nine to ten knots. Great sailing!

Meanwhile, Jim left the hospital in San Luis Obispo, and flew to Seattle. We hoped he could join us for at least part of the sail north.

Then it started raining and the temperature dropped. We sailed into Coos Bay, Oregon, under poor visibility in the rain. I called the harbormaster on the VHF radio about the condition of the bar at the harbor entrance, and he said it was safe to enter.

The harbor was filled with hundreds of big fishing boats. We spent the day drying out the boat and cleaning up. I bought a chart of the Columbia River mouth. We took nice hot showers, which was a great pleasure after several days of no showers. I talked with some of the local fishermen about Newport and Tillamook, and they thought we could safely enter the harbors with our draft. We cooked up a chicken dinner to celebrate arriving in Oregon and passing halfway from San Diego to Seattle.

At 5:30 AM we headed out of the channel in the usual parade of fishing boats. Then all of a sudden, the boats ahead of us stopped and lay over on an angle; they had run aground. It was a bit unnerving. Four boats were aground on our left, and another six were aground on our right. I crossed my fingers, and very slowly went through the middle. We touched bottom, and my heart sank, but then we were off, and on our way.

We arrived at Newport, Oregon, after motoring all day in light air on calm seas. We went to the fuel dock and got some fuel, and then left Newport for Tillamook. There was a little wind, so we motor sailed with just the main up. The cutting of the trees was very noticeable here. Whole mountainsides had been denuded.

When we arrived at Tillamook Harbor, the Coast Guard came out to greet us and tell us the best way in through the bar. We went to the boat basin at Garibaldi and were shown to a nice slip by the harbormaster. This bay has a dangerous entrance bar, so I called the Coast Guard to find out the best time to leave in the morning, and they said within the next two hours, so we packed up and left at midnight.

The weather was cold and drizzly, but we sailed all night any way. In the morning we sighted the Columbia River Lightship, and what seemed to be about a million small fishing boats outside the mouth the river. It was Sunday, and all the local fishermen were out.

The Columbia River bar is infamous. It has killed hundreds of seamen over the years. On an ebb tide and big seas, the waves can reach fifty feet and break right across the entrance.

Luckily, the bar wasn't breaking with large waves, and we were able to make it into Astoria. We went into the small boat harbor in Astoria and got a berth. There were a lot of people coming by to see the boat. Jim, the owner, arrived from Bremerton, with his parents, Don and Beth.

We filled up with fuel at the fuel dock and left Astoria at 8:00 AM. It rained all the way out the river and across the bar. We had a nice wind for about an hour, and then it died. We motored all the way to Gray's Harbor. Westport and Gray's Harbor are completely filled with charter fishing boats, and people come from all over Washington to go fishing in the ocean here. The whole town consists of fishing charter offices, motels, and restaurants for the tourists. The people on the boat next to ours gave us a nice salmon, and we cooked it up for dinner.

We left Gray's Harbor and motored up the coast of Washington. We went through the middle of a huge fishing fleet and put out our lines with no luck. The sun came out, the wind filled in and came aft, so we put up the spinnaker and had a beautiful sail all afternoon. We saw our first sailboat since leaving San Francisco.

We went into La Push for the night. It's a nice little Indian village set in the trees of the Olympic Forest. It's really a beautiful spot.

We left La Push with the morning parade of fishing boats in cold and foggy conditions. Near Cape Flattery, the fog really closed in, and we could only see about fifty feet. We slowed the boat way down; after a lot of careful navigation, and some tense moments, we rounded Tatoosh Island, and headed into Neah Bay. We had now sailed the entire West Coast of the continental United States.

We tied up to the fuel dock in Neah Bay and bought a salmon from fishermen for dinner. Neah Bay is another Indian village on an alcohol-free Indian reservation, so we had to wait another day to celebrate.

We left Neah Bay early in the morning for Port Townsend, motoring on the American side of the Juan de Fuca Strait. We enjoyed the view of a beautiful coastline with tall trees coming right down to the water's edge. The sun was bright, and the Strait was flat and calm. The wind came up as we passed Port Angeles, so we put up the spinnaker and really started moving, especially with the help of the flood tide. We were doing about eleven knots over the bottom. We arrived at Port Townsend about 11:00 PM, took a walk into town to have a look around, and then went to bed.

Port Townsend is a pretty little town, rebuilt from the old buildings that were once used to build ships. We walked up the hills to see all the old restored vintage 1850s homes. It is quite a lovely area.

We cast off for Seattle, sailing down an inland passage, through the

Oak Bay Canal, and then out into Puget Sound. It was a pleasant sail across the Sound to Shilshole Marina, *Barefoot's* new home in Seattle.

Jim's friend, Donna Gay Stirrett, asked me if I would like to visit Bremerton, across Puget Sound from Seattle, for a couple days. I took her up on her offer, and she arranged for me to stay at her mother's house on Holly Horse Farm. The farm was stunningly beautiful, overlooking the water. Her mother, Ethel Lent, was wonderful; she treated me like a son. It was the highlight of my trip and started a wonderful friendship that has lasted thirty years.

Holly Horse Farm, Bremerton, Washington

Four

Outrageous –
Transpac 1977

Fifty-foot Tom Wylie-designed sloop
Owner/Skipper/Doctor—Dr. Ted Burns
Crew: John Jourdane, Mark Laura, Perry Jones, Dick Hershberger, Roger Johnson,
Keith Dearborn, Bill Walgren, John Kern, R. K. Beers

When I was in Bremerton with *Barefoot*, Donna Gay Stirrett introduced me to Dr. Ted Burns, a dentist from Bremerton, who was building a new fifty-foot Tom Wylie-designed sloop to race in Puget Sound and in the Transpac race to Hawaii. I went to Bainbridge Island and saw the boat under construction. It was quite beautiful, built of diagonally laminated cedar strips, and covered in fiberglass.

Ted offered me a paid position as navigator for the Transpac Race from Los Angeles to Hawaii the next July, and also for the delivery back to Bremerton. It took me less than a minute to think about it and say I was available. He said the boat was doing the Swiftsure Race in Victoria to tune up for Transpac. He wanted me to fly to Seattle and meet him on the boat at the Seattle Yacht Club.

I went to the Yacht Club and saw the boat. It was new with shiny black topsides, a gray deck, and a very tall mast. No one was aboard, so I tossed my duffel on deck and climbed aboard. The boat wasn't locked, and I went below to have a look around.

Outrageous at the Seattle Yacht Club

While I was checking out the accommodations, there was a knock on the hull, so I went on deck expecting to find Ted. Instead there were two gentlemen in black suits carrying brief cases. They said they were from the Internal Revenue Service, and that the boat had been seized by the IRS for nonpayment of back taxes. They proceeded to tape a sign on the topsides which read, "Property of the U.S. Internal Revenue Service." They brought out a chain and locked the boat to the dock. My first exposure to *Outrageous* wasn't going well.

Ted arrived, took a look at the signs, and said, "Don't worry, this is a mistake. My lawyer will straighten this out." Ted went to the phone, and I prepared the boat for the delivery to Victoria for the Swiftsure Race.

Somehow the lawyer did straighten it out, and Ted and I left for Victoria the next day. As we were clearing locks from Lake Union to Puget Sound, it started snowing. It was May, and I had just come from Hawaii, where I sailed in the warm tropical trade winds, and I had to ask myself, "What am I doing here." I've asked myself that question many times over the last forty-five years of sailing.

We motored *Outrageous* to Port Townsend, spent the night there, and then continued on to Victoria, where we met the race crew. The Swiftsure Race is notoriously rough. It starts with a light reach or run through Race Passage, then a light beat out the Strait of Juan de Fuca. But as the afternoon turns to evening, the winds build, and you sail into the North Pacific Ocean to a ship anchored several miles off the mouth of the strait. The ship is anchored on the spot where the old Swiftsure Lightship used to be anchored. Once you get out into the Pacific, it gets very rough, with strong winds and huge waves.

The race went as well as we could expect. We didn't win; it was a shake-down sail. Several things broke or didn't work, and we found lots of leaks that had to be sealed before Transpac, but we survived without any great problems.

I delivered the boat from Bremerton to Los Angeles for the start of the Transpac race. We had a good crew aboard including Sandy Pensinger, who had helped me deliver *Barefoot* from San Diego to Bremerton, and my brother Tom. It was a pleasant voyage down the coast, covering the 900 miles in six days.

The 1977 Transpac Race was quite windy, with vicious black rain squalls in the middle of pitch black nights. *Outrageous* was a very light boat with a lot of sail area, designed to race in the light winds of Puget Sound. Steering the boat with the spinnaker up in a lot of wind was a handful, and we broached many times, rounding up, and then rounding down. I remember saying after the race that I thought we were the first boat to sail to Hawaii on our side.

The navigation station was located across the boat from the galley, and I often had a ham or a pot of spaghetti land on my chart as I was trying to navigate.

We had the newest navigation instrument aboard, called Omega. It received radio signals from Omega stations around the Pacific Ocean, and gave us a constant line of position. The only problem was you had to tell it where you started, and then it would track your course as you sailed. When the batteries got too low, it would lose power, and I had to initialize it all over again. To initialize it, I had to use my sextant to give me a current sight, then use that sight to program the Omega. But the Omega kept going out, so I really navigated the whole race to Honolulu with the sextant. But somehow we found Hawaii, and the finish line off Diamond Head, and had many great stories to tell over many mai tais.

The 1977 Transpac was a very memorable race in that it was the fastest ever up to that time. Five boats beat the elapsed time record, including *Merlin*, whose time of eight days and eleven hours stood for twenty years. It was also one of the windiest races ever. This was made possible by the position of the Pacific high. It was about 400 miles east of its normal summer position, at 38°N and 145°W. This squeezed the isobars between it and the low over Nevada, causing strong winds for most the race.

In the early morning hours of day seven, a series of squalls hit the fleet with winds from thirty-five to forty knots and large seas from behind. A total of five boats lost their masts. They were *Concubine*, a Cal 40; *Mistress III*, a Tartan 41; *Incredible*, a Peterson 41; *Nimble*, a 42-foot sloop; and *Nalu IV*, a Lapworth 48. All five boats managed to set up jury rigs of various kinds and continued racing. They even started their own class, the "Broken Mast Class," and had a race amongst themselves. The winner in that class even received a trophy when they reached Hawaii.

Some of the 52 Japanese glass balls we collected

It was a wild ride to Hawaii on *Outrageous*, and we blew up most of our spinnakers. But the arrival in Honolulu made it all worth while. As we sailed past Koko Head and approached the finish line off Diamond Head, we started smelling the flowers. Then when we arrived at the Ala Wai Boat Harbor, we were greeted by hundreds of friends and well-wishers. We were greeted by Hawaiian music, hula dancers, and great quantities of mai tais on the dock. After a few drinks, we forgot the bad parts of the race and started talking about doing the race again in two years.

My brother Tom flew to Honolulu to join me for the delivery back to Bremerton, Washington. We had a fun, leisurely, thirteen-day sail back to the West Coast. Our course took us right through the middle of the North Pacific high. We beat north for six days, and then motored across the calm high and through a lot of flotsam, where we caught quite a few mahimahi.

I think we set the world's record for collecting Japanese glass floats. Tom would sit up in the spreaders with binoculars and look for glass balls, and the crew would steer the boat all over the ocean, and scoop them up in a large salmon net. By the time I made them stop, because we were running low on fuel, we had collected fifty-two glass balls.

We stopped the boat in the middle of the high and took down sails and all jumped in the flat, calm water for a swim. It was strange to dive down into the colder water below the surface, and know that it was over 20,000 feet deep. We were at a spot farther from land than anywhere on earth.

We also saw a UFO. It was a bright turquoise ball of light that crossed over us from west to the east, from horizon to horizon in less than two minutes. I still have no idea what it was. But it makes for a great story.

Tom driving and John navigating

After thirteen days, we sighted Cape Flattery, and sailed past Tatoosh Island and into the Strait of Juan de Fuca. We anchored off Neah Bay and went ashore for some cold beers, but remembered that Neah Bay is an Indian reservation and there is no alcohol allowed. But there was a local salmon fishing boat anchored near us, and when we told them we had just sailed in from Hawaii, they gave us a nice salmon and a couple six packs of beer, and we celebrated our arrival.

Five

Hattie Mai Aloha
Brian Keith's Boat—
Ventura to Honolulu

In March 1979, after several months of sailing in Hawaii, I received a phone call from Don Miller, a yacht broker in New Jersey, asking if I would be interested in delivering a 41-foot ketch from Oxnard, California, to Honolulu for actor Brian Keith. I called around, and started finding crew. My brother Tom was interested, and Arleone Dibbens, an experienced sailor whom I'd met in Marina del Rey, wanted to go as well. A man named Roy Allen, whom I'd met in Honolulu but didn't know very well, accepted.

I flew from Honolulu to Los Angeles, then drove north to Oxnard, and found the boat in the Channel Islands Marina. It was an Island Trader 41 ketch. The boat was big and beautiful, but I sensed problems. It was built in Taiwan, and at the time, Taiwanese boats didn't have the best reputation for quality.

When I got to the boat, the diesel mechanic, Homer, was busily working on it. It seemed that the electrical system had shorted and burned up. Homer was replacing all the wires on the boat. The alternator had also burned out.

Hattie Mai Aloha in the Channel Islands Marina

Tom and Arleone showed up, but not Roy. Tom and Arleone set out to buy provisions. I went through the boat with Chris Buchanan, who had done the commissioning when the boat arrived from China. It was a brand new boat.

Actor Buddy Ebsen came by with his skipper, Jack Holmes. Since Brian Keith was in Hawaii, he asked Buddy to help us get the boat ready for sea. Buddy was an outstanding sailor and had done very well racing his catamaran, *Polynesian Concept,* up and down the West Coast and to Hawaii. Buddy and Jack made a list of things they felt we should have on the boat, and opened up an account for us at the chandlery. It was *carte blanche*—we could order anything we felt the boat needed.

I went up the mast to check the rigging. We got a phone call from Roy. He was at the Los Angeles Airport with six dollars, not enough to get to Oxnard on the bus. He had been there since 3:00 PM the day before, so Tom drove down to get him, and brought him up to Oxnard. Arleone was working out great! She was a good organizer, and a nonstop, hard worker.

The people at the Marina were very friendly and helpful. Al in the chandlery was great, always taking the time to help us with our needs or give us advice on which item he felt was better for the job. The weather report said a big rainstorm was coming in. We might have to wait a few days to leave. I sent Tom all over town to find a weather map, but he had no luck. The Oxnard Airport said, "We don't get weather reports, we just go outside and take our own observations." Roy wasn't getting involved in the preparation; he was just sitting around on the boat, then going for walks around the marina.

It rained pretty heavily that night, and we found a lot of leaks in the deck. It would make for an interesting trip. Tom, Arleone, and I had a meeting, and decided Roy wasn't working out. Arleone had a friend named Steve, who would be willing to take Roy's place on the crew. So I sat down with Roy, and told him he was off the crew, and I would pay his way back to Honolulu.

We left Buchanan Yacht Sales in the Channel Islands Marina at 7:00 AM. The trip from Oxnard to Marina Del Rey went very smoothly. We put up a full mainsail and the large Genoa. The wind kept building all afternoon. By the time we arrived at Marina Del Rey at 3:00 PM, it was blowing about twenty-five knots out of the Southwest; a sure sign that a front was moving in.

We woke up at 5:00 AM to a cold rain and decided to leave anyway. The boat was ready, and we had our full crew, so, we sent Roy off to the airport and left the dock at 7:00 AM for Honolulu.

Our new crew man was Steve Lewis. He seemed like a good man. Not a very experienced sailor, but very enthusiastic and easy-going. Steve was a film producer who lived in Hollywood.

We put up the mainsail and the large jib, and were reaching along at good speed when the port jib track lifted off the deck. I hoped it was not a sign of the craftsmanship of the whole boat. The track was held onto the cap rail by wood screws instead of being through-bolted, as it should have been. We lashed the metal rail down, moved the jib car to the middle of the track, and kept sailing.

We passed the west end of Santa Catalina Island at noon, and as the sun went down, we could make out San Clemente Island, which we passed by during the night. This was the last land we would see until we reached Hawaii.

During the night, Tom saw a lot of blinking red lights in the skies, so he called me up on deck. We saw flares and gunfire. The Navy must have been playing war games off San Clemente Island. I just hoped they didn't think we were a target.

It was a cold night, but at least the watches were short. We weren't used to the routine or the motion of the boat yet, and no one got much sleep. I tried using the refrigerator battery to start the engine, and it worked, so we had a spare battery. Homer's rheostat charging system seemed to be working well. The steering system made a lot of noise, but was working. I would try bleeding the hydraulic line in the morning.

There was a cold wind blowing from the north. I told everyone we would be in the trade winds in a couple days, and it would warm up. The sea became a bit more organized, and everyone was feeling better. I still hadn't figured out a good way to get any sleep in my bunk. It was sideways across the aft cabin, and as the boat rolled, I alternately got my feet and then my head pushed against the sides of the hull.

April Fools' Day! The sun had come out at last. I was able to get some good sun shots with the sextant and do some navigation. We were moving right along, doing better than 150 miles a day. The boat was pretty fast on a reach, which we had been doing since Catalina.

I managed to get a good morning shot with the sextant, and then went to work on the engine. We were getting water in the fuel separator. I tore out the floor boards and found a drain in the fuel tanks. The first tank didn't have any water in it, but the second one did. I found about ten to fifteen gallons of water in the bilge; it must have come in through the fuel vent in the stanchion. The engine started fine after bleeding the lines. I took my first saltwater shower. It was cold, but it felt great, and very refreshing. I felt like a new man (at least I smelled like a new man).

The wind finally came around from the northwest, and we put up the large genoa that Buddy Ebsen had given us from his aforementioned famous catamaran, *Polynesian Concept*. The sail fit our boat very well, and we went "wing-and-wing" with the mainsail out on one side of the boat and a jib held out on the other side with a spinnaker pole. An albatross visited us for a while. Its wingspan must have been about six feet. Some consider the albatross a sign of bad luck, but I have seen one or more on every ocean crossing, and I consider them good luck.

The wind was nonexistent, so we motored. The whole crew took showers on that nice, sunny morning. They were cold saltwater showers, but they really felt quite good. We were visited by a white tropical bird with a long tail. He tried to land on our mast for couple of hours, then gave up and flew away. It clouded over and was cool in the afternoon. There was still no wind. The engine died; more water in the fuel, so we shut down the fuel tank that had water and closed it off. We had no problems after that.

We motored all night, and still had no wind in the morning. Where were the trade winds? We motored all day and still found no wind. Either we were in the North Pacific high, or the high wasn't strong enough to make trade winds. It was cloudy and cool, and there was a lot of debris floating by, plastic, Styrofoam, buckets, etc...The engine was dying every half-hour so. Air was getting into the fuel lines.

We were halfway to Hawaii, and still hadn't found the trade winds. It was very calm and sunny. We finally fixed the engine. We were just too low on fuel in the tank. We added fuel from the jerry cans, and that seemed to have solved the problem. We dropped the sails, and went for a swim. The sea was calm and flat, and the swim felt really refreshing. It was the highlight of the trip to that point. The wind finally filled in during the afternoon. We stopped motoring and put up some sails.

We had a festive half way dinner of ham sandwiches and champagne. The day was topped off with a beautiful sunset, with a half moon and a starry sky. We were sailing along quietly and smoothly at about five knots.

The trade winds finally arrived. The weather was sunny with about twenty knots of wind coming from behind, and we had large following seas. I gave Steve instructions in steering in following seas so we didn't broach or accidentally jibe. The last several days had been calm, and we had to get used to the motion all over again. The boat was moving right along downwind. We were doing six to seven knots steady. She sailed well with the wind on the beam or aft of the beam, but I don't think I would want to have to sail her too far into the wind.

We started getting lots of squalls during the night, with gusts to about thirty knots. We put two reefs in the main during the night and then put up a small jib. The boat surfed a few times, and hit twelve knots on the knot meter.

Big crisis! We were out of bread. No more peanut butter and jelly sandwiches. The squalls kept coming through all day; it was sunny for a while, and then raining like crazy, and then sunny again. We caught a nice mahimahi, cooked in cashews, onions, and olive oil, and had it for dinner. It was delicious!

The wind died, so we shook the reefs out of the main and put up a bigger jib. It was cleaning day. We scrubbed down the teak and fiberglass above decks and cleaned the interior. Everyone took a shower. A clean boat is a happy boat!

Tom and I played skeet shooting with the rotting apples and oranges. One of us would throw up a fruit in the air and the other would try to hit it with another piece of fruit. It was great fun.

Previous page: Hattie Mai Aloha at sea.

Scoundrels at sea; John, Tom and Steve

We woke up to rain and no wind. The sun eventually came out, but still no wind. Land ho! We sighted Kalaupapa Light on Molokai. We motored past Ilio Point, and the Molokai channel was like a mirror; very unusual. We passed Makapuu Point around noon, and Diamond Head 2:00 PM.

We arrived at the marina, and were greeted by Brian Keith and his family with a cooler of ice cold beers. Brian was very happy with the boat and the crew and congratulated us for a quick crossing.

We spent the next day cleaning up the boat then sailed across the Molokai Channel with Brian Keith aboard, around the island of Lanai to Lahaina on Maui. There we were met by Buddy Ebsen, who was going to use the boat for filming a TV movie called *The Paradise Connection*. It was about a famous Chicago criminal lawyer, Stuart Douglas (Ebsen), who arrives on Maui searching for his son, Bruce, played by Brian Kerwin, who has run away from a promising legal career. It appears that Bruce has become involved in a dangerous drug smuggling operation. Anyway, Buddy hired me to skipper the boat for the filming.

They put me up in a fine hotel, and each day a limousine would pick me up and drive me to Lahaina yacht harbor where I would get the boat ready for the day's filming. I would drive the boat around, and duck below, whenever they filmed one of the actors steering. It was great fun, and they paid me a lot of money for sailing around Lahaina. The best part of the job was sailing the boat back to Honolulu with Buddy Ebsen. We spent the whole day sailing downwind in the trade winds and sharing sea stories. He was a top notch sailor and a genuinely nice man.

Six

Genesis

San Pedro, California, to Kahului, Maui, Hawaii, on an old fishing trawler – 1979

I received a call from Mike Keeler, who asked me if I was interested in helping him deliver his 38-foot Kettenburg trawler from San Pedro to Maui. I thought about it for a while, then said, "Why not, it will be an adventure."

I flew to Los Angeles, and met Mike and his dad, Willard, on the boat in San Pedro. We went through the boat and engine, and then powered to Catalina for a shake-down. The boat seemed plenty sturdy, but it did roll a lot with the wind and waves on the beam. It was built in Monterey in 1944 and was used for decades as a commercial fishing boat in Monterey. Mike bought it to use in Hawaii for the same purpose.

Our third crewman, Dave joined us, and we spent the morning running around getting spare engine parts, and loading up with every tool we could possibly need. The boat only had one engine, and that was a bit of a worry. If we lost the engine, it was a long drift to Hawaii.

Genesis in San Pedro, California

We went to the fuel dock, and loaded on 2,000 gallons of diesel fuel, and a lot of engine oil. We said goodbye to Mr. and Mrs. Keeler, cast off from Fish Harbor in San Pedro, and headed north. We stopped in Marina Del Rey for dinner, and then motored north to Channel Islands Marina in Oxnard, where we went shopping for last minute items, cleaned the boat, and took our last hot showers.

We left Oxnard, and headed out through the Channel Islands. The wind and seas were quite calm in the lee of the islands. We caught a nice albacore and put it in the live bait tank until dinner. The wind and sea picked up once we cleared the islands. The autopilot started acting up; it couldn't handle the big, steep, confused seas. In spite of the rough seas, we had a great albacore and pork and beans dinner.

The wind picked up to twenty-five knots from the northwest, and the seas were about twelve feet. The boat rolled a lot in the seas, but it seemed to handle it fine. We headed downwind at noon so I could take a noon sight with the sextant, and we added oil to the engine. The starting battery was overcharging and was very hot to the touch. We took it out of the system until we could find the problem.

I was getting plenty of sleep, because there wasn't much to do in the rough seas except steer the boat and sleep. We had canned stew for dinner; it was easy to cook and easy on the stomach.

The first morning out of Oxnard dawned with sunny skies and fairly calm seas. It gave us a chance to clean up the boat. A rain squall came through in the afternoon, and we all took salt water showers on the aft deck, with a rain water rinse. We started having more battery problems. Both main batteries were overcharging, and the starting battery seemed ruined, so we spent the afternoon changing alternators. Then when we tried the new alternator, it would not charge at all, so we removed the new alternator, and put the old one back on with a new voltage regulator. It was still overcharging, so we decided to manually charge each main battery one hour a day, then unhook it from the alternator. It was a pain in the butt, but at least we had charged batteries.

The wind built to twenty-five knots with twelve-foot seas. I felt like I was back in the Molokai Channel. The boat rolled over in the troughs and felt like it was going to keep going, and capsize, but it always came right back up, and steered the proper course. It was designed for the rough seas off Northern California.

The boats motion was very uncomfortable. The seas were hitting us on the beam, and the boat rolled through forty-five degrees to port, then forty-five degrees to starboard. The wind was still from the north, so the North Pacific high must have been ahead of us. We were trying to get to the high and its calm waters.

We caught a nice mahimahi, and had it for dinner. It was a good sign. Mahimahi are found in the tropics, so we must have been getting closer to the trade winds.

We shut down the engine to change the fuel and oil filters. I was a little apprehensive about doing it, because our batteries were not in the best shape, and we might not be able to start the engine again. We cranked the engine over as everyone held their breath and crossed their fingers, and it started right up.

The number two and number three bilge pumps quit working, so we were pumping the whole boat with the number one pump. We had covered almost 700 miles, all of it in heavy wind and seas. We would have loved this weather in the last Transpac Race, but it was calm all the way. Now we wanted calm seas and no wind, but couldn't find them. I think it is a corollary to "Murphy's Law:" The wind and sea conditions you get are inversely proportional to the conditions you want!

Finally, we had a beautiful sunny day. The wind and seas were still up, but the sun was out and I could use my sextant to find out where we were. We caught a nice bull mahimahi, and had a great fish dinner.

We had used all the fuel in the 55 gallon drums lashed on deck, so we stowed them below, and had a lot more room on deck.

We were half way to Maui, and it finally was calming down. We had about ten knots of wind and four- to six-foot seas. Dave developed a bad rash all over his body. We didn't know what caused it, but it seemed to be getting worse. I gave him some Benadryl, thinking it might be an allergy. We started seeing a lot of flotsam—plastic bottles, Styrofoam, and so forth—so I guessed we must be nearing the High. The North Pacific High is like a giant whirlpool and much of the trash floating in the Pacific slowly drifts inward toward the center of the High.

The autopilot started acting up again. We steered the boat manually during to day to conserve our autopilot bulbs, which kept burning out.

We lost four fish and two lures, but finally caught a nice mahimahi just after Mike had cooked spaghetti for dinner. We put the fish on ice until the next day.

Finding out where we are.

Genesis tied up at the Matson Dock in Kahalui Harbor.

We finally found the North Pacific high. It became very calm, with flat, mirror-like seas. It was a perfect day for taking care of the boat. We spent the day changing the oil, fuel and oil filters, and transferred fuel into the starboard tank. We also replaced the broken bilge pumps in the fish hold.

We all soaped up and dove into the water for a swim. It felt great! Then we climbed to the top of the mast and dove off as the boat rolled from side to side.

We awoke to a glassy sea and sunny skies. "Yes, Virginia, there is a North Pacific high." We had a beautiful, clear night, perfect for star-gazing, and I managed to work out a really nice three-star fix with the sextant, using Sirius, Pollux, and Alpharatz.

We had a ship pass by about two miles to starboard during the night. This morning we picked up two glass balls, and caught a nice mahimahi. It was almost surreal; the fish came skipping across the surface, then made a ninety degree turn, and headed straight for our lure. Then, bam! He was on the line.

The next day was calm, sunny, and hot. We caught a mahimahi early in the morning. We must have been traveling at a good fishing speed, because we caught fish almost every day of the trip.

In the afternoon, we sighted a very strange collection of ships. There was a very large ship, like an aircraft carrier, and six or seven smaller ships. They were all in a circle facing each other. As we approached, a U.S. Navy helicopter took off, and came toward us, waving us off. I don't know what was going on, and I wasn't going to stick around and find out. We altered course, and gave them a wide berth.

In the afternoon, we stopped and went for a swim. The water was warm and clear. It was a bit strange thinking that the nearest "land" was about three miles straight down.

The calm weather stayed with us. We appreciated it after the first part of the voyage. The cabin was really hot, so I slept out on the stern deck, where it was quite pleasant.

We caught another mahimahi. That made seven mahimahi and several albacore and bonita we had pulled aboard. I still enjoyed the fish and looked forward to eating it each evening.

A big aircraft carrier steamed by, then a Navy helicopter came over and buzzed us a few times. I picked up Honolulu weather on the radio, and they said we should have light air and calm seas for the next couple days. That was good news! I slept on deck under the stars again.

We caught two more mahimahi in the morning, and let one go. We seemed to catch them in pairs. It was another calm day with flat seas. The second half of the trip turned out to be the opposite of the first half, weather-wise. We encountered no trade winds. We were getting near land, and the crew was restless. We sighted the lights on Maui about 2:00 AM. We had sighted Kula and Makawao on the slopes of Haleakala. I also picked up the lumen of the Molokai Lighthouse off to starboard. At dawn, we could see Haleakala, the west end of Maui, and Molokai very clearly.

We pulled into Kahului harbor in the morning. We were met by Mike's wife, Peggy Ward, and some ice cold champagne.

The S&S 49, Tuia

Seven

Tuia

Los Angeles to Tahiti Race — 1978

Owner— Bob and Nancy Gosnell
Crew—Bob Dickson, John Jourdane, Woodii Carr, John Hundhammer,
Jeff Sherman, John Anderson, Brian Carter.

I met Bob and Nancy Gosnell in Tahiti in 1974. They had raced their ketch, *Spirit*, in the Los Angeles to Tahiti Race. A year later they purchased *Aura*, a very successful Sparkman and Stephens 49-footer. She had a very successful racing career on the East Coast. They sailed her to California, and renamed her *Tuia*, and were going to race her in the 1978 Los Angeles to Tahiti Race. Bob and Nancy asked me to join their crew and meet the boat at the Newport Harbor Yacht Club in Newport Beach, California. I flew in from Honolulu, and we spent a couple days practicing off Newport Beach. The boat was tied up at the Yacht Club, and most the crew were sleeping aboard.

The night before the race started, John Hundhammer, Woodii Carr, and I had a few drinks at the club, and then went out for dinner and a few more drinks. We stayed out a "little late," and when we tried to get in the Yacht Club (and our bunks), we found it completely dark and locked up, and there was no security guard or anyone around to let us in. I said we should just climb over the fence, which was about eight feet tall, and Woodii, who is African American, said, "Are you crazy, this is

Newport Beach, they would take one look at me, a black man climbing
into Newport Harbor Yacht Club in the middle of the night, and they
would shoot first, and ask questions later." So, we walked and found a
small hotel, managed to survive, and made it to the boat in the morning.

The race was a pleasant sail, reaching under spinnaker most of the
3,500 miles, except for a few light and variable days in the Doldrums with
a lot of rain squalls interspersed between the calms. We were pretty
evenly matched with another fifty-footer in the race called *Westward*.
Willard Bell and his whole family sailed the boat out of Los Angeles
Yacht Club. They were all seasoned ocean racers and gave us all we could
handle. In a long ocean race like this one, you often never see another
boat after the start. Having *Westward* nearby made the race much more
interesting.

Our sailing master for the race was Bob Dickson. This was the first
time I had sailed with him, but we would sail together again and again.
Bob is one of the legends of Pacific Ocean racing, having crossed the
Pacific so many times on so many boats, he can't remember. He is not
only a great sailor and seaman, but a true gentleman. Many of the important things I learned about sailing offshore, I learned from Bob.

One evening, in the Doldrums, we were on deck as the sun went
down, having a "happy hour," and telling lies to the other watch. The
calm sea exploded with jets of water, and we were attacked by squid.
Using their jet propulsion, they flew out of the water, and hit the crew,
the sails, and landed on the deck, squirting purple ink all over. We ran
around the deck picking the slimy creatures up, and threw them back into
the sea. Nancy ran on deck and yelled, "Save them, I'll cook them for
dinner!" So, instead of throwing them back, we put them in the pot,
and ended up collecting over twenty l squid, about 18 inches long, and
Nancy made a great calamari dinner.

As we approached the equator, Woodii started complaining about his
bunk. He said it smelled awful, and we all said ours did too, after 2

weeks at sea. He kept complaining, so we all went to his bunk, and said it smelled the same as ours. Every day, Woodii would say the same, all the way to Tahiti, and we just laughed it off as a too-sensitive nose. When we did arrive in Papeete, we took the boat apart, and scrubbed it out. We found a dead, very rotten flying fish in the Dorade vent right over Woodii's head.

On the twenty-first day of the race, we were nearing the finish line and were in a good position to beat *Sorcery*, a 61-foot C&C design owned by Jake Wood, on handicap time. *Sorcery* had finished several days earlier, but with the handicap rating, we could still beat her. But as we neared the island, the wind died. We had twelve hours to go twelve miles to win on corrected time. We sat off Point Venus in a mirror like sea, and we could see the finish line, but we were slowly drifting backward in an adverse current. Jake rented a power boat, and came out to welcome us. He gave us cold beers, circled us, and watched the time run out. It was frustrating, but Jake was a good sport, and we had a great time with the *Sorcery* crew in Tahiti.

The Bali Hai Yacht Race

After about a week in Papeete, we sailed to Moorea to participate in the Bali Hai Yacht Race. It was one of the most unforgettable races I have been in. The yachts all anchored off the Bali Hai Hotel, and the crews attended a great luau. The next morning, the crews of all the boats gathered around tables on the beach, and had to drink a sixteen-ounce mai tai (or virgin mai tai for the kids). Then all the crews had finished their drinks and turned it over, they ran to the water, dove in and swam to their boats. They then hoisted the anchor, and motored out the channel in the reef. Once clear of the reef, they hoisted sails, and headed for the island of Huahine, some 100 miles away. It was an overnight race, and we had several Tahitians aboard, who played ukulele, drank rum, sang, and even danced on the bucking deck all night long.

Bob and Nancy had a Tahitian friend, Roto, who was along for his local knowledge for the race. Roto was a former captain of Tahitian trading ships and spoke very little English. He knew only three phrases, but it was enough English for any occasion: "No problem, captain;" "Big problem, captain;" and "Bullshit, shut up."

In the morning we sailed into Huahine, lowered sails, and motored through the channel in the reef. We pulled up to the beach in front of the Bali Hai Hotel Huahine. I had to dive off the boat, swim to the beach, then run to the bar, where I had to drink another sixteen-ounce Mai Tai, turn my glass over, and compute our time for the race.

We arrived at the beach at the same time as *Westward*, and as I ran up the beach and into the bar, who should show up but Rosie Bell. We picked up our drinks and started to chug them, when we both choked. It was sixteen ounces of pure rum! It turned out the owner of Bali Hai Hotels, Hugh Kelly, was on *Sorcery*, and had beaten us to the finish. He was behind the bar laughing as we tried to drink the pure alcohol. I turned to Rosie, and said, "We can't drink this, it will kill us." She said, "Drink it, and we'll both go outside and throw it up." We did both, and we became close friends from then on. Hugh said we were such good sports that all our drinks and food for the night were on the house. It was a wild night, with another luau, drinking and dancing, and I don't know what else. I woke up the next morning in a hammock on the beach.

The Bali Hai Hotel in Huahine

Bahia Mar, at anchor in the Bahamas

Eight

Race Passage

Victoria-Maui Race, Clipper Cup, Honolulu to Victoria to Stuart Island, British Columbia to Bremerton, Washington

Owner/Skipper—Dr. Paul McCullough
Crew: John Jourdane, Robin Fleming, John Ward, Roger Bright, Perk Sherer, Dale Jensen, and Ross Caniglia

Donna Gay Stirrett introduced me to Dr. Paul McCullough, who owned a new Swan 441, called *Race Passage*. He had won the Vic-Maui Race a couple years earlier on his Swan 44, also named *Race Passage*, and he needed a navigator and delivery skipper for the next 1980 Vic-Maui Race. I signed on.

I spent the month of June at the Shilshole Marina in Seattle getting the boat ready for the race. We hauled her out, checked the mast and rigging, and tore down all the winches and blocks.

I delivered the boat in a cold, dreary rain up Puget Sound to Victoria, British Columbia, on Vancouver Island. We went through customs and immigration, then moved to the Inner Harbour, where we dropped an anchor and tied up stern-to in front of the Empress Hotel.

The next day, the crew all arrived. I attended the Skipper's Meeting with Paul, then we had a nice crew dinner.

Deck of Race Passage in Shilshole Marina, Seattle

The race started at 10:00 AM in about twenty-five knots of wind. It was wild. We crossed the starting line prematurely, and had to sail back and restart. We sailed out Race Passage, the entrance to Victoria and the name-sake of the boat, and started beating out the Strait of Juan de Fuca to the Pacific Ocean.

We were the sixth boat around Tatoosh Island, behind *Triumph, Glory, Indomitable, Chiron,* and *Scaramouche.*

I went to the bow to help change sails, and got my christening by the Pacific. A big wave broke over us, and I was completely soaked in cold sea water. We cracked sheets and set the #1 jib top and staysail, and sailed all night at a comfortable 8.5 knots of boat speed. By the second day, the sky had cleared, the wind came aft, and we put up a spinnaker and tall stay-sail. The seas settled down, and we were moving along at 9.5 knots.

On day three, the wind built to twenty to twenty-five knots, and we were doing a steady ten knots, with surfs to fourteen. At roll call, we were the third boat in the fleet behind the 70-foot *Min Sette* and the 61-foot *Triumph*. *Glory* had dropped out with rudder problems; it was heading to San Francisco.

The *Race Passage* crew was really good. Everyone was low key, knowledgeable, and good helmsmen. We had no yelling or tension on the boat. The maneuvers all went smoothly and nothing broke.

On day four, the wind died and we changed to the light air sails. We were visited by a pod of Pacific white-sided dolphins. At roll call, we were in third place behind *Triumph* and *Chiron*.

Ross made us a great spaghetti dinner served with his own homemade wine. Every year he buys a tank car of California grapes and bottles his own cabernet and zinfandel in Iowa.

On day five, the weather map looked bleak. There was a big high pressure ridge forming right across our path to Maui. We had our slowest average speed so far, 3.5 knots for an hour. We sighted a boat dead ahead of us, sailed hard all day, and slowly caught up to them. It was *Chiron*, and we steadily sailed away from them, with a lot of dolphin, jumping and playing in our bow wave.

Day seven was the Fourth of July, and Mother Nature supplied some fireworks. We sailed through several big rain squalls, some with lightning. There was a lot of wind in front of the squalls, but no wind behind them.

We were rewarded with a Fourth of July present at roll call. We were leading the fleet boat for boat. It was hard to believe that after six days, the big boats hadn't passed us, but we weren't complaining.

Day eight gave us more rain squalls with a mixture of wind and calms. We sighted a boat off to port, and it turned out to be *Chiron* again. It looked like we were going to be racing them to the finish.

Day ten found us in steady trade winds with sunny skies, and puffy cumulus clouds. It turned into a boat cleanup day, and then we all took salt water showers.

Kanata was now the lead boat. It had snuck down from the west side of the High; an unusual move, but it worked. The fleet had closed up, and it looked like a close race for first boat to finish between *Kanata, Chiron, Wizard, Triumph,* and us.

Skipper, Dr. Paul McCullough at the helm

Day twelve gave us a morning of rain and windy squalls. We blew out the blooper, and spent most the day taping and sewing it back together. We were in second place again, this time behind *Chiron.* Paul splurged and shared his vodka with the crew. We had a pleasant happy hour with vodka tonics on the "veranda."

Day thirteen was hot and sunny after a very rough and squally night. We blew out the blooper again, and it flew from the masthead like pennant for several hours before we could get it down. We were in first place again, but *Triumph* hadn't reported in for several days, and they were probably in the lead. We saw a large boat go by us during the night, and it was probably *Triumph.*

We crossed the finish line in Lahaina, Maui, at 4:00 AM. We were the third boat to finish. *Triumph* had beaten us in, and *Chiron* snuck by again to cross just ahead of us. But we won Class A on corrected time.

Race Passage crosses the finish line in Lahaina

Clipper Cup

Crew: Paul McCullough, John Jourdane, Dick Deaver, Tim Rhea,
Woodii Carr, Les Vasconcellos, Skip Winterbottom, Danny McFaull,
Charlie Isaacs, Kirk Denebeim, and Frank Beering.

The Clipper Cup was one of the best regattas in the world. The race was well run, the courses were great, the wind was a steady fifteen to twenty-five knots, the water was warm, and ice cold mai tais were served after every race. Paul had decided to enter Clipper Cup, and do the first four races, but because of time constraints, not the Around the State Race.

Dick Deaver came aboard and took charge. We practiced, tuned the rigging, marked all the sheet leads, retuned the rig, re-marked all the leads, labeled all the winches, marked all the halyards, and put scales on the mast and deck to note halyard tension. Dick was very thorough; that is why he won so many races.

The first race was around the island of Oahu. The race took the fleet from the starting line off Diamond Head and down the leeward side of the island to Kaena Point. It was a fast reach under spinnaker to the point, then the wind lightened until we got around to Haleiwa. We beat back up to Kailua in a fresh breeze, rounded Koko Head, and ran to the finish off Diamond Head. We managed sixth place.

The next three races were Olympic Triangles off Waikiki. It was exciting sailing in the twenty knot trade winds, but *Race Passage* just had too much furniture aboard and couldn't really compete with the stripped-out race machines. We ended up in the middle of the fleet, but we had a lot of fun and some great sailing.

Honolulu to Vancouver Island

We motored to the fuel dock, and loaded on diesel, then left the Ala Wai Yacht Harbor, and sailed down the island to Pokai Bay where we anchored and had dinner, took a nap, then headed out past Kaena Point.

The trade winds were blowing twenty to twenty-five knots, so we put a reef in the main, hoisted the #4 jib, and headed north. The boat had an autopilot, and it worked well under sail or power. It was like having an extra crewman, whom we called "Otto." Bob was pretty seasick, but we were sure he would get over it in a couple days. Nick, Dan, and I were rotating, taking Bob's watch for him.

We beat north for day after day, looking for the wind to lighten as we approached the North Pacific high. But the wind kept blowing, and I kept saying, "Tomorrow we should be near the high." But the next day it was still blowing. It continued day after day, until the crew didn't believe there was a high.

Finally, after eight days of sailing north, the wind died, and the seas flattened out. We were at latitude 42 degrees North (abeam Oregon). I had described to the crew how we would stop and go swimming in the high. So we soaped up and dove in. The water was very cold, but it still felt good. Even Bob had gotten out of his bunk and seemed alive. The calm only lasted two days, then we hit the Westerlies, and the wind steadily increased to gale force. The good thing was it was from behind, and we put a reef in the main and wung out a blast reacher. We were sailing quickly toward Vancouver Island.

Bob became sick again and went back to his bunk. He was not having a very good time on the voyage. The wind abated after a couple days, and the last couple days into the coast were beautiful. We had calm seas, clear skies, and a full moon.

We rounded Cape Flattery and motored into Neah Bay. Bob, jumped out of his bunk, got his sea bag, and ran off the boat so fast, we almost

couldn't say good bye. It was an easy sail to Victoria, where we went
through customs. I called Paul to let him know we arrived, and he asked
me if I would take the boat up through the Canadian San Juan Islands
to Stuart Island. We day-sailed the boat from Vancouver to Ganges on
Saltspring Island to Pender Harbor to Lund to the Copeland Islands to
Stuart Island. The scenery was breathtaking; high mountains covered
with firs and cedars that grow right down to the water's edge.

Paul flew to Stuart Island on a seaplane with some buddies to go
salmon fishing. The crew and I flew out on the plane, which landed in
front of Paul's waterfront home in Bremerton. He had given me the keys
to his house and car and said make myself at home. I stayed in the house
for a week, and visited my friends Donna Gay Stirrett and Ethel Lent at
Holly Horse Farm. Then the seaplane landed in front of Paul's, and flew
Paul's son and me to Stuart Island. Paul and his friends flew out with a
cooler full of salmon, and we delivered the boat down the San Juan Islands
and Puget Sound to *Race Passage*'s home at the Bremerton Yacht Club.

Motoring through the Canadian San Juan Islands

Nine

Ondine
SORC – Southern Ocean Racing Circuit

I met Sumner "Huey" Long in Honolulu after a Transpac Race in the early seventies. His skipper, Frank Crane, was kind enough to give me a tour of *Ondine*, a 79-foot Britton Chance design built of aluminum by Derecktors Boatyard in New York. It was a huge boat, with a 100-foot mast, painted light blue, as all the previous *Ondines* had been. The boat was quite nicely fitted out below. It had staterooms for all the crew, a dining table that seated twelve, and separate navigator's and owner's staterooms. The boat even had a sauna. As I left, I gave him my card and said, "If he should need crew in the future, please give me a call." In the Fall of 1980 I received that call from Mr. Long, asking me if I would like to sail on *Ondine* in the 1980 SORC.

SORC was a series of six races off southern Florida. The first was from St. Petersburg to Boca Grande and back to St. Petersburg. The second was from St. Petersburg around the bottom of Florida to Fort Lauderdale. The third race was the Ocean Triangle Race, which goes from Fort Lauderdale to Great Isaac Cay to Palm Beach to Miami. The fourth race was the Lipton Cup, from Miami to Gun Cay to Fort Lauderdale to Miami. The fifth Race was from Miami to Nassau, Bahamas. The sixth race was an Olympic Triangle off Nassau.

I flew to St. Petersburg, Florida, and met the boat at the St. Petersburg Yacht Club. As I boarded, I received a list of "*Ondine* Rules." They included: There will be no swearing aboard the boat, no whistling is allowed, no food or drink is to be eaten on deck, no alcohol, no cookies or candy (sugar is bad for you), you must put your sheets, blankets, and pillows in a special case after sleeping, all crew gear will be kept in the crewman's sea bag, or will be thrown out, and you must call the owner Mr. Long or Skipper, never Huey.

Ondine racing in the SORC

The first race was the Boca Grande Race. It was a wild start in heavy air, gusting to thirty knots. We were the second boat under the Skyway Bridge, behind *Kialoa*. It rained heavily all night with lots of a thunder and lightning, lots of squalls, and a whole lot of sail changes. The really hard part of sailing on *Ondine* was moving the sails—they were huge. The luffs were 100 feet, it took six men to lift one of the genoas, and the spinnakers had to be packed into 100-foot snakes.

I was working hard on the foredeck. We were doing a lot of sail changes; most were without anticipation of what the wind would be doing next and which sail would be going up next.

It lightened up around midnight, and we just flogged around a lot. It became very foggy in the morning. Ted Turner's *Tenacious* came out of the fog, about thirty yards away, and crossed our bow. The wind came up during the morning and was back up to thirty knots by noon. We finished fourth behind *Kialoa*, *Mistress Quickly*, and *Boomerang*. We felt we did okay since we had no crew practice and our only crew meeting was on the way to the starting line.

The second race was the St. Petersburg to Fort Lauderdale Race, a 180-miler in the Gulf Stream. The weather at the start of the race was beautiful, sunny, and warm. We had a great spinnaker run all night with a full moon and speeds up to eighteen knots. We rounded Rebecca Shoals about 9:00 AM, and the wind came around on the nose as we rounded the bottom of Florida. We reached out into the favorable current of the Gulf Stream, and I got to do some driving. The boat was very easy to steer. I was able to keep her at eleven knots to weather steering with one hand. We were abeam the *Kialoa* for the lead when the wind lightened, and she slowly pulled ahead. We finished second.

In the third race, The Ocean Triangle, we finished in second place. In the fourth race, the Lipton Cup, we finished third. We finished fourth in race five, the Miami-Nassau Race, and we finished sixth in race six, the Nassau Cup. The boat was not as fast as *Kialoa*, and we made a lot of mistakes, but we had a lot of fun, and I learned a lot about sailing maxis.

I offered to help deliver the boat back to Miami, and it turned out to be more than I bargained for. We left Nassau in the morning, and had a wonderful spinnaker run under clear, sunny skies to Bond's Cay. We anchored, went for a swim, and had a party.

It was my birthday, and we had a great dinner with lots of rum. We weighed anchor at 9:00 PM and headed for Stirrup Cay under a clear, starry night with almost no wind. As we passed Great Isaac Cay in the morning, the wind freshened, and we were doing a steady 10.5 knots to weather. The boat seemed to go faster cruising than it did racing.

It was another beautiful day sailing across the Gulf Stream. We were carried north by the Stream, so we had to tack down the beach to Miami. We were running low on fuel as we entered Miami, so we put up the genoa and tacked up the shipping channel. As we turned the corner into Miamarina, we went hard aground. Our beautiful cruise home from Nassau was turning sour. We put everyone on the bow, and tried to power off, but the boat didn't budge, and the engine died. A small power boat came by, and we threw them a line. They tried pulling us off with no success. We put all the crew out on the boom and had the powerboat pull, still no movement.

Finally, we took a line from our spinnaker halyard to the dock, and winched the masthead over while the powerboat pulled. Success! We got off the bottom and coasted into the dock with no power. But what had started as an easy sail had become quite a trial. We tied up, fired up the Mount Gay rums and orange juice, and finally relaxed, telling *Ondine* stories.

Buenos Aires to Rio de Janeiro Race

I must not have made too bad of an impression on Mr. Long, because a couple months later, he called and asked me if I would like to race *Ondine* in the Buenos Aires to Rio de Janeiro Race. The boat was for sale, and the Brazilian navy was interested in buying it. They wanted to use the race as trial sail. I jumped at the chance, and booked my flight from Los Angeles to Rio de Janeiro the same day.

The flight turned out to be quite an adventure. I flew five hours from Los Angeles to New York, then had a four-hour layover, followed by nine hours to Rio de Janeiro, then a one-hour layover in Rio, followed by three more hours on the flight to Buenos Aires. Of course, it didn't go that easy. I arrived in Buenos Aires, and as I tried to clear customs, they said they would not let me into the country, because I did not have a visa into Argentina from Brazil. I would have to go back to Rio on the next flight.

This was something out of a Franz Kafka novel. I needed a visa to get into Argentina from Brazil, but I didn't have one, because I didn't need one to get into Argentina from the United States. I didn't really go into Brazil, because I did not deplane in Rio. The same plane continued to Buenos Aires. I had two separate tickets, a round-trip from Los Angeles to Rio, and a one-way ticket from Rio to Buenos Aires. So theoretically, I stopped in Rio, and needed a visa to get into Argentina. I was quite mixed up.

Needless to say, I had to take the next flight back to Rio. If it wasn't so funny and so "South American," I would have been mad. Luckily I still had four days until the start of the Buenos Aires to Rio race.

It got even weirder as I tried to explain to the Brazilian customs agent why I didn't have a customs clearance from Argentina. Somehow, they let me in to Rio, and I caught a cab to the Hotel Regina. The problem now was to find the Argentinean Consulate and try to get a visa quickly, then catch a flight back to Buenos Aires. The saga continued. I went to Pan Am to book the flight to Buenos Aires, and they said the first one they could get me on was in two weeks. The race started in three days.

They did tell me where the Argentinean Consulate was located, and I headed over there. When I arrived at the Consulate, they were closed; their hours were noon to 5 PM. I went back to the Consulate at noon, and they wouldn't let me in the front door, because I had shorts on. So I walked back to my hotel and put on slacks and a blazer, and walked back to the Consulate in the hot Brazilian summer sun. They finally let me in the Consulate and said I could pick up my visa at 4 PM the following day.

With that taken care of, I then concentrated on my next problem; getting to Buenos Aires before the race started on Saturday. After going to Varig, LAN Chile, and Avianca Airlines, I finally got on a flight the next evening at 7:20 PM on Aerolineas Argentinas. It was a tight schedule. I hoped my visa was ready at 4 PM. It was really hot in Rio, much hotter than Hawaii. There are no trade winds to cool off the sun's heat, so I spent the afternoon on the beach swimming and walking around the bay, watching the "Girls from Ipanema."

I got up early and had some breakfast. It came with the room, and consisted of a hard boiled egg, coffee, orange juice, and bread, and also a plate of papaya, banana, and watermelon. I checked out of my room and paid my bill. It was 3,850 cruzeiros, for two nights, or about $55 US. Not too bad, considering everything else in Rio was very expensive.

I only had to wait a half hour for my visa at the Argentine consulate. I caught a bus back downtown to Dumont Airport, then the airport bus to Galeao Airport. When I came into Rio in the middle of the night, I had to get a taxi into town, and that cost 1,000 cruzeiros. The airport bus was only 70 cruzeiros. "You live and learn."

I arrived in Buenos Aires again, and they let me in their country. But it was midnight, and there were no airport buses running. It was twenty-one miles into town, and a taxi cost $56 US. I asked a janitor at the airport if there was a public bus that went into town. He said, "Yes, catch bus number 86 out by the gas station." So I walked out to the gas station, waited an hour, and caught bus number 86. I asked the bus driver if it went to downtown Buenos Aires. He said no, it went to Linares, but it was near downtown. So at two o'clock in the morning I went to Linares. It turned out Linares was nowhere near downtown, but it was a lot closer than the airport, so I got off the bus and caught a cab, which took me to a hotel. So I ended up at the Hotel Rochester in downtown Buenos Aires at 3 AM. I took a shower and got a couple hours sleep.

I caught a taxi and told the driver to take me to Yacht Club D'Arsena. He'd never heard of it, but we drove to the part of town called D'Arsena, and were given directions to the Club de Pesca (fishing club), then we went to the various docks, until I finally saw a very tall mast, which turned out to be *Ondine*'s. The boat was hauled out at the navy shipyard.

It was like "old home week," when I arrived at the boat. Eric de Bakker from Holland was there, Dave Berridge from New Zealand, and Tom Corness from Canada was the new skipper. Richard Todd and Steve Schenk were there, also. All of them were on the boat in the SORC races in Florida.

We spent the day putting away the provisions, cleaning the bottom, and generally getting the boat ready for the race. The boat was out of the water on a submersible dry dock. And the dockworkers were having problems getting it back in the water. When they started sinking the dry dock, it caught on a concrete pier, and they had to bring in welders with cutting torches to make it sink. We finally got back into the water and took the boat to Yacht Club de Argentina. We had showers, a turkey dinner on board, and beers at the club bar, than it was bedtime. The race started the next day.

We got up early and got to work packing the sails. We left the dock at 11:00 AM, even though the start wasn't until 3:00 PM. We motored around, put up the mainsail, and dodged the spectator fleet. Thirty-five boats were racing, but there must have been a thousand spectator boats with hundreds of beautiful bikini-clad Argentine women aboard. This drove our crew to distraction.

It was really hard sailing through the spectator fleet. All kinds and sizes of vessels surrounded us, and some were even anchored right on the starting line. As we were approaching the line for the start, a big 70-foot ketch, named *Juana II*, started coming down on us with no rights. We kept yelling, "Come up," but they didn't seem to understand the English, and we hit each other. They didn't hit us hard, but we had to put up the protest flag because they made contact. We had a terrible start at the wrong end of the line, and we were three minutes late.

We managed, however, to pass the fleet and took the lead, as we sailed out of the Rio Plata. We were patting ourselves on the back, and then we went hard aground in the mud. We had a navigator aboard from the Argentine navy. We also had an admiral from the Argentine navy and an Admiral from the Brazilian navy aboard. That tells me something about the Argentine and Brazilian navies. We had to put up a spinnaker and put everyone out on the boom, and finally, we got off the mud. It was strange to be sailing in a muddy river. It's incredibly large. We couldn't see land, but we had to sail 200 miles in it to get to the Atlantic Ocean.

We had light winds in the afternoon, about eight knots, and then the wind picked up to about twenty knots in the evening. Then we had a period of calm. Then a couple squalls came through with about thirty-five to forty knots of wind, but it got light again. In the morning, we saw a long band of clouds, white at the top and black at the bottom. It approached very quickly, and the Argentine sailors said it was what they call a "Pampero," and we must shorten sail quickly. We put two reefs in the mainsail, and put up with the number two jib top. There was calm, and then the wind came aft and gusted to fifty knots. It wasn't as bad as we had expected, so we put up the small spinnaker.

The crew was working out really well. They were a great bunch of guys—really international—we had twenty-one crew members aboard from ten different countries. After the big squall, the wind came aft, the sun came out, and we started sailing really fast. We averaged better than eleven knots all day, and hit fifteen knots a couple of times while surfing. It was almost like sailing the Transpac Race to Hawaii.

Our twenty-four-hour run was 226 miles. Not bad considering we were going to weather for part of that, were aground for a while, and had a couple of calm periods. We had our first daily bulletin from Mr. Long, stating our miles made good, distance to go, average speed, ETA, and a list of rules like; "the crew must shave or trim their beards daily", "the crew must keep their personal gear put away," and so on. In the afternoon, I had a nice one-on-one talk with Mr. Long. It was the first time I had spent time with him, and found him to be very articulate and quite interesting.

All the local sailors aboard said we should have been beating into the wind at this point in the race, but we still had our spinnaker up. This was not normal, but we weren't complaining. It was sunny and hot, the seas were flat, and we were averaging ten knots over the ground. If this kept up, we would have a very fast trip. The record for elapsed time for this race was over seven days by a boat named *Saga*. At this rate we would finish in less than six days. The race is 1200 miles long, and we had covered over 450 miles in two days.

The admiral from Argentina had brought aboard a huge cask of red wine as a present, not knowing Mr. Long's rule about no alcohol, and when the crew saw it, they hid it in the galley. We were served a red Kool-Aid-like drink called "bug juice" at every meal. The admiral was a rascal, and played along with us, and each evening served those who wanted it great Argentine red wine instead of "bug juice" at each meal. If Huey knew, he never let on. This was turning out to be a memorable sail on *Ondine*.

The wind lightened during the night. It became even lighter the next day, with many calms and the wind and boat speed displays showing all zeroes. We were very frustrated after sailing in the good winds we had experienced to that point. But the weather was beautiful; it was really hot and sunny, and everyone was in good spirits. Steering was very difficult when there was no wind. By the time the sun went down, the wind started filling back in, and we went through a lot of sail changes. The wind stayed with us through the night. We were rewarded with great home-baked lasagna for dinner. We had roast beef, chicken, steaks, and fresh salads and vegetables for dinner; pancakes, eggs, and omelets for breakfast, and chili, chorizos, and quiches for lunch. I was getting fat.

The wind held, but we were on an LFTO. That means "Lightning Fast Tack to Oblivion," or the helmsman was sailing in the wrong direction. But it was a beautiful sunny day, again with the wind out of the east at about ten knots. We finally tacked, and were heading for the finish line, about 400 miles away.

I spent my free time, when I wasn't steering, learning some new knots from Peter, who was in the Swedish navy. It was really a little United Nations aboard, and fun to hear so many different views of the world. In the evening the wind picked up, and we put in the first reef, then the second reef, and as it got stronger we went to the number three genoa. We had a joke-telling time during the night watch. Hernan told some great Argentinean jokes, Peter told some Swedish jokes, Phil offered up some British jokes, and I pitched in a few "Portagee" jokes from Hawaii.

The wind built to about thirty knots, and we experienced short, steep chop. Mr. Long came on deck and told us to shake out the reefs. There was too much wind to do that, but we did it anyway, he owned the boat. About two minutes later, he was shouting for us to put the reefs back in. Oh well, "that's sailing." We were taking some fairly big seas over the bow. I got off watch and found that someone had opened the port over my bunk, and it was soaking wet. At least it was hot and the water was warm.

The wind was coming right out of Rio, so we had to tack to get there. It was really frustrating not to be able to sail closer to the rhumb line. If we could have sailed straight to Rio, we could beat the elapsed time record without much trouble, but we had to sail a lot farther by tacking. We were all hoping for a wind shift. A jib sheet snapped under the heavy load, and it was 5/16 inch wire. That's a lot of pressure on those sails. I kept my distance from all sheets, guys, and blocks that were under load, they could kill me. The wind kept building, and we went to the number four jib and three reefs in the main. It was really a wild night. We were down to four reefs in the main and the storm forestaysail. The wind was a steady forty knots, and gusting to fifty. The headboard on the main sail blew out, and we had to take down the main and put up the storm trysail. Steering was really difficult. The seas were about twenty feet high, and it was like driving an obstacle course around and over the waves, to try to keep from falling off the tops and crashing down. There was no moon; it was pitch-black. You only knew when a big wave was coming in by seeing the phosphorescence of the breaking tops. During all this we kept the boat moving at about ten knots to weather. These were the conditions for which the boat was designed. *Ondine* sailed beautifully to weather in big seas. As dawn slowly lightened the eastern sky, the wind died down. We repaired the mainsail, and put it back up.

We crossed the finish line at 1:00 in the morning, beating the elapsed time record by thirteen hours. It was a bad time to finish because it was 3:30 AM by the time we reached the Rio Yacht Club; no one was there to greet us. But it was a very sweet victory, because we knew we had done so well. It was *Ondine's* last race under Mr. Long's ownership, and we all felt a little sad to leave her. She had shown her mettle. It was a race that tested the boat and crew, with all conditions of wind and sea. We had gone through the entire sail inventory, eighty-four sail changes in all, and we prevailed. It was a race to be proud of. Good sailing, good racing, good crew, and good friends.

Richard Wells one of our crew, had promised the crew that he would buy us five cases of beer if we beat the record. He made good his promise, and we proceeded to get quite drunk. In Brazil, the case of beer has forty-eight cans. The second boat *Fortuna*, finished the late in the afternoon, and we partied with them, then had a nice dinner at the Rio Yacht Club, and went to bed early.

Ondine in Rio de Janeiro

The Brazilian navy did decide to purchase the boat, and we stayed in Rio for a couple weeks to help the midshipmen learn how to sail a maxi. It was quite an experience. It was also *Carnival* in Rio, and the city went mad. We would sail all day, then drink and dance most the night. It was hard, exhausting duty, be we were young and managed to handle the challenge.

Language was a big problem when we were trying to teach the Brazilians—most of them spoke no English, had not sailed before, and didn't know the difference between a sheet, a guy, and a halyard. They wore tight Speedo swim suits and were constantly singing and dancing the Samba as we sailed. *Ondine* is a big, powerful sailboat, and we were afraid something would break, and someone would get killed. Finally, when we left them, we said, "See these sheets that are not made of wire? They go with the smaller sails. Just use these sheets and the smaller sails."

Ondine's Europe Adventure

After the Buenos Aires to Rio Race, Mr. Long asked me if I was interested in working as crew on the new *Ondine*, which was being built at that time at Palmer Johnson Shipyard in Sturgeon Bay, Wisconsin. The boat would sail to Europe and race in the Maxi World Championships in Sardinia. It sounded like a great adventure, and I signed on.

I flew to Wisconsin in May, and moved into the crew house, a nice cabin about ten miles north of town. It was located on the shores of Clark Lake and had a beautiful view. Sturgeon Bay is a ship-building town, and many of the bulk ore carriers plying the Great Lakes are built there. The local people were very friendly and had noticeable Swedish-Midwestern accents. They were also very pale and nonoriental, which was quite different from Hawaii, where I had lived for the past 10 years. The first morning there, I ran into town from our cabin, and it started snowing on me. This was very different from Hawaii!

I went to Palmer Johnson to check out the boat, and it was quite unusual. It was either going to be very fast or a "real dog." It looked kind of like an 80-foot Laser, really flat on the bottom, and it had a wide transom. It was light for an 80-foot aluminum boat, weighing only 73,000 pounds. I was a little worried about it being made of 1/8 inch aluminum plate. That's pretty thin.

Palmer Johnson wouldn't let us on the boat during working hours, so we spent the mornings at a beach near our house. It was summer, and the days were hot and sunny. But the water in Lake Michigan was very cold, about 45°F. I had some great runs out in the country, passing picture perfect farms with classic barns and silos full of grain.

We worked at Palmer Johnson in the afternoons, cleaning up the construction debris, and doing some painting and varnishing. After work we would go to the Pro Lounge, which turned into the crew's local drinking hole.

The Ondine crew van in Wisconsin

We started putting the spreaders and shrouds on the mast. We measured the angles on the spreaders. Five out of six came out perfect, but one was off. No matter what we tried, we couldn't get it to measure and look quite right. Don Kasten, from PJ came over, looked down the mast, and said "Take three turns on the L-1." We did, and the mast looked perfect.

Mr. Long arrived with his wife Suzanne, and Russell, his son. We moved the boat out of the shed, and Suzanne christened it. Then we put it in the water to see how high it floated, and it floated really high.

We bought a keg of beer for the guys in the yard, and joined them for a launching party. Just when we were patting ourselves on a job well done, Jerry Milgram, the designer, received a phone call from the USYRU Rating Office telling him the boat was illegal, and would rate about 80 feet. We couldn't race IOR with a rating over 70 feet. So we had a big problem.

Mr. Long took us out to lunch, and told us we were going to make the Seahorse Maxi Series in Cowes, England. To do it, we had to leave Sturgeon Bay by Monday, June 29, and make it to England in twenty days. I think the fastest trip ever from Sturgeon Bay to England was by Jim Kilroy's *Kialoa*, in 22 days. So we had our work cut out for us. Huey said we also had to be in Oslo, Norway on August 17 for a reception with King Olav and Crown Prince Harald of Norway. That meant we had to leave England as soon as we finished the Fastnet Race, then we had to average ten knots to weather all away to Norway. We would only be in Norway a day or two, then leave for the Mediterranean and Sardinia.

I went to see a doctor about getting some drugs for the medical kit. It was pretty funny. Before they would let me see the doctor, the nurse had to take my weight, pulse, and blood pressure. I kept telling her I was just there for a consultation, and she kept saying if I wanted to see the doctor, she had to take my weight, pulse, and blood pressure. So, I was weighed and had my pulse and blood pressure checked.

We put *Ondine* in the water. Then we put in the mast for the first time. It was really tall and very flexible, kind of like a noodle. We spent the day lubricating the winches and blocks and anything that moved. That afternoon, Kevin, one of the workers at Palmer Johnson, put on a fish boil at our cottage. He brought a big pot and a propane torch. He filled the pot with boiled potatoes and onions and trout. It was fabulous! A lot of the Palmer Johnson workers came by, and we spent the evening swapping boat-building stories.

It was a pleasant break from all the tension swirling around the boat.

The next day was *Ondine*'s first sea trial. Mr. Long and Dr. Milgram came along, and we headed out on Green Bay to do her first sailing. When we hoisted the sails, the boat tipped over, and the mast almost went in the water, and there was only about ten knots of wind. Not a good sign! The boat was way too tender. And the backstay was too long, so we couldn't get enough mast bend. As a result, there was way too much headstay sag. The rig was very complicated, with several running back-stays, making it very difficult to tack. We motored back to Palmer Johnson with a long list of things to fix.

The crew all went to a pig roast at the Gardner Gun Club. It was really fun. They had trap shooting, country music, and really good food. We got to meet nonsailing Sturgeon Bay folk, and they were quite friendly, especially the young women.

A few days later we went sailing again. The wind was very light, and the boat sailed well. David Vietor came out on a power boat, looked at our sails, and then came aboard. A big rain squall came through, and I watched it on the radar. It was quite visible on the radar. A piece of infor-mation I would use many times in the future. The boat had some prob-lems with the folding propeller. There was a piece of small line wrapped around it, so Kiwi Dave jumped into the freezing water and cut it off. It was the biggest folding propeller ever made; 42 inches across and it weighed 170 pounds.

Right: Ondine sailing on Green Bay, Wisconsin

I drove into Green Bay to pick up Eric de Bakker. It was good to have Eric back aboard. He really knows maxi racers, and could tell Huey what had to be done to get the boat on the right track. I took Eric to the boat, and he was pretty amazed at how different the boat was from all the other maxis on the racing circuit.

Lieutenant Eric De Bakker of the Dutch Navy

We went up to Bailey's Harbor, and I ran a Fourth of July 10K race with Dave, Tom, and his girlfriend Maureen. It was hot and sunny, and the course was like a cross-country run over a golf course. We stayed in Bailey's Harbor all day for a Fourth of July parade and fair. It was a lot of fun seeing the Fourth of July celebrated in "Middle America." It was so much more festive and patriotic than I've seen on the West Coast or Hawaii. We went to The home of Palmer Johnson's rigger, Scotty, for a really nice dinner and fireworks. Scottie's house is a beautiful 100-year-old stone estate on the water with impeccably landscaped grounds. It was a nice evening with steaks, a keg of beer, and music. Eric de Bakker played some beautiful classical piano interspersed with a bit of Ragtime.

Scottie Turner came to Palmer Johnson as crew on the yacht *Stormvogel*. He got a job at Palmer Johnson as a rigger, married the owner's daughter, and now owns half the company. He still works as a rigger when he wants to. He says, "When I came over the Sturgeon Bay Bridge, I had seventy-five cents in my pocket and all my possessions over my shoulder. Now I can buy the damn bridge." He is quite a character, but a great sailor and a really nice guy.

After weeks of delay, we finally left Palmer Johnson. Hooray! We slowly motored out the Sturgeon Bay Canal and into Lake Michigan. It was a beautiful, calm night. We would motor all-night until we reached Mackinaw Island, then try sailing. The boat had seventeen people aboard; most were only going to Detroit, and then getting off. The paid crew that would sail to Europe were: Tom Corness, the skipper; David Berridge, John Jourdane, Eric de Bakker, Phil Barrett, Charlie Roach, and Sally Crane, our cook.

As we sailed through Gray's Reef Passage and under the Mackinaw Bridge, a big weather system came through, and it rained like crazy. We found a lot of leaks, especially a big one right over my bunk. We slowly started putting the gear away, and could actually walk around inside the boat. We sailed all day down Lake Huron under sunny skies. The water was dark blue, and quite clean. We tried several different sails during the afternoon, and sailed most of the night with a cruising reacher sail up.

We sailed into Port Huron, got some fuel, and then powered down the St. Clair River. It was really scenic, with beautiful homes along the water's edge. There were a lot of people going down the river on inner tubes; long lines of them hooked to together with coolers full of beer. It looked like a lot of fun.

We crossed Lake St. Clair, and were met by Richard Todd on a power-boat. He took us to the Detroit Yacht Club, where there was a really nice reception for us with cold champagne, an open bar, and lots of pretty girls. But we only got to stay for two hours, and then had to leave. Several crew got off in Detroit, and we picked up Dave Holmes and Keith Lorence from the North Sails Loft in Detroit. As we were leaving Detroit, we went aground in the Detroit River. It was *Ondine's* first grounding. It was mud, and we got off pretty easily, but it was not her last grounding. We entered Lake Erie, and headed for Port Colborne, Canada, where the boat would be officially handed over to Mr. Long by Palmer Johnson in Canadian waters. By purchasing the boat in Canada, Mr. Long would save a lot of money by avoiding sales tax.

As we sailed across Lake Erie, we were attacked by lake flies. They are black and aggressive, and they bite! I must have killed thousands. We made it through the flies to Port Colborne, and started into the Welland Canal. There are eight locks between Lake Erie and Lake Ontario, and the only way down is over Niagara Falls or through the canal. We chose the canal.

We passed through all eight locks with no problem. Each lock was a drop of only a few feet. A lot of large ships were heading the other way going up the locks into Lake Erie. Some of them are built to just fit in the locks, exactly 727 ft. long, and the same length as the locks. It took us about six hours to get through all the locks, which was quite fast. Usually it takes eight to twelve hours. There wasn't much traffic going down, and we didn't have to wait. It was a wet, dismal day as we powered across Lake Ontario. We set up galley duty and a meal schedule. It rained pretty heavily as we left Lake Ontario and entered the St. Lawrence Seaway. There was a small black object on the foredeck, and when I went to throw it over, it turned out to be a very wet bat. I dried it off, and put it in a box with some rags, and it stayed with us for a couple days, and then flew off to a less bouncy place.

We passed through the Thousand Islands area of the Saint Lawrence. There were incredible mansions built on the islands. Several looked like castles straight out of Disneyland. The river is very narrow here, and we were passing ships heading up the river as we were heading down. Navigation is quite tricky. There are buoys and course changes every few hundred yards. The St. Lawrence Seaway Control was following us all the way, along with all the other ships. We had to check in every few miles with the Control. We also had a two knot current going with us, so we were moving along pretty fast.

We powered all day down the St. Lawrence past what seemed like millions of buoys, and then through another eight locks. We had to wait three and a half hours at the last lock to let us into Montreal.

We tied up in the Ile Saint Helene Marina in Montreal, and spent the evening at La Ronde, an amusement park adjacent to the Marina.

We worked on the boat frantically getting ready to sail. Tom went to the airport to pick up our mainsail, which had been shipped in by Hood sails, and also some additional gear sent by Palmer Johnson. We took on a new crewman, Rodney Holland from North Carolina. We hit a rock pretty hard leaving the marina in Montreal. Charlie dove down to inspect the damage. It wasn't bad, so we continued down the river to Quebec.

We powered all night down the river and passed Quebec shortly after dawn. Quebec looks really beautiful from the water, with a skyline of ancient buildings and churches along side sleek modern office buildings. The wind came aft and increased, so we set the mainsail. A strong current was running, giving us good speed down the river. We set the 2.2 ounce spinnaker, and were doing eleven knots plus three to four knots of current. We were flying down the river. The water temperature dropped from seventy-two degrees near Quebec to forty-five degrees as we approached the ocean.

It was a calm night, so we took down the spinnaker and started motoring. We powered all morning along the Gaspe Peninsula. We were now in the Gulf of St. Lawrence, and needed some wind to make it to England in time for the Fastnet Race. The maps coming through on the weather fax said we should be hit by a cold front the next day.

The wind came up during the night, and we sailed on a close reach with the cruising reacher up, doing ten to eleven knots. The wind held all morning at about twenty to twenty-five knots. It was a sunny day; really good sailing. We were treated to a beautiful night of northern lights and a sky full of stars as we reached along with the number two genoa.

We pulled into the small island of Saint-Pierre. It's a quiet little fishing island with brightly colored buildings and just as brightly colored fishing boats. We fixed the head foil, which had opened up, repaired a couple of holes in the reacher, and topped off the fuel and water tanks.

We went to the local hotel pub for a lightning fast beer, and found it was jammed with young ladies. It turned out that the University of Toronto has a French language school here. Saint-Pierre is a territory of France, not Canada, and French is the spoken language. There must have been a couple hundred girls from the University. We had a few more beers and gave a lot of tours of our boat to the young ladies.

When we left Saint-Pierre at about 5:00 AM, it was raining. Outside the harbor the rain and wind built, and it blew a steady twenty-five to thirty-five knots with eight to ten foot seas. We were finding a lot of leaks in the deck. The one-half-inch Lexan companionway washboard broke when it was slammed shut. One of the heads was broken. We had diesel oil in the bilge, and it smelled quite bad down below. I had the feeling I'd been here before. The front passed through, and the wind clocked to the west. Visibility was poor with a lot of fog. We were keeping a constant radar watch for ships.

Something snapped in the drive train of the engine, so we shut it down, and had no propulsion. We changed course and sailed toward St. John's harbor in Newfoundland. When I called the Coast Guard to ask for a tow into St. John's harbor, they said they didn't have a boat available, "Fend for yourselves." So we hailed a fishing boat, and they towed us in.

St. John's is a really large city tucked away in the coastline. You can't see it until you get into the harbor itself. It is the easternmost city in North America. We tied up to some crab boats in the harbor and went through customs and immigration. There was a bar right across the street, so the whole crew went in with full foul weather gear and harnesses on. We clipped our harnesses to the brass rail around the bar, and said, "Hold on, there's a rum squall coming!"

We cleaned the boat and fixed some of the major leaks. A local guy, named Bill Buckley, came by, and it turned out he used to skipper *Sorcery* for Jake Wood in California. He was a big help in getting our phone calls through, and lining up engine repair. We even got to take hot showers at his apartment. Bill took us to the local hotspot, the Sundance Saloon. It was good fun. The Sundance was a western bar, so we all had a few drinks, did a lot of dancing, and rode the mechanical bull. It was a nice release after all problems on the boat. I met a local schoolteacher named Renee. Like me, she was a biology teacher, so we had a lot in common.

The next day Renee took me on a tour of St. John's. We went out to a marine laboratory on the coast, and to Signal Hill, where Marconi sent the first wireless message to Europe. The view of the city was awesome. It's quite large, once you leave the harbor. We drove around town, and then went with the crew to a local pub, the Fishing Admiral, for a few lightning-fast beers.

St. John's has the best-looking women in one place I've ever seen. It's a five to one ratio of women to men, because the men are all out fishing on the Grand Banks or off on mainland Canada, where they can find jobs. It's not a bad place to be stranded for repairs.

As much as we liked St. John's, we had to get going, or we wouldn't make the King's party in Norway. So, we cast off early on a beautiful, calm, sunny morning. It was a bit sad leaving St. John's and all our new friends. As we left the harbor, several whales came by to send us off. We also had to negotiate our way through several crab boats and a maze of crab pot buoys. We put up the 2.2 ounce reaching spinnaker, and we were on our way to Norway. Everyone was really tired. We all had a little too much fun in St. John's. It would take us a few days to "dry" out.

I got the sextant out, and started taking sights. After our first day out, our position was: 49° 22' North, 47° 44' West, 225 miles out of Newfoundland; 2,155 miles to Oslo. We were passing over the Grand Banks, and it became quite foggy. There were a lot of targets on the radar. We were in the fishing grounds.

Scoundrels Filthy Phil Barrett and David Berridge

Day 2 out: Noon sight: 51° 23' N, 43° 10' W; 436 miles out; 1,922 miles to Oslo; day's run: 213 miles. We put up the big 2.2 ounce spinnaker during the night, and we averaged ten knots for 24 hours. It was nice to be sailing without the engine noise.

A tropical depression, Cindy, was moving toward us from the southwest. It clouded over and started raining in the evening. We were sailing fast under the 2.2 ounce chute, when we almost hit a huge whale, about 60 feet long, it seemed to be sleeping, and didn't even move as we flew by.

Day 3: Noon sight: 53° 14' N, 37° 39' W; 663 miles out; 1,696 miles to Oslo; day's run: 227 miles. It was a cold and rainy morning, and we were moving along at eleven knots under the big 2.5 ounce spinnaker. This was the real north Atlantic I'd heard about, dark and gloomy with big seas. The wind came forward, and *Ondine* suffered her first knockdown. We took the chute down and put up the reacher. The barometer was dropping pretty fast. The wind kept coming forward and backed around to the east, then northeast, then north, and then it picked up to thirty knots. The boat was doing 12.5 knots with just a small reaching jib up.

Day 4: Noon sight: 54° 24' N, 31° 42' W; 883 miles out; 1,476 miles to Oslo; day's run: 220 miles. The wind increased and backed. We had the storm forestaysail up and a reefed main, and we were doing eleven knots. It was getting cold, and the only place you could get warm was in your bunk.

Day 5: Noon sight: 55° 59' N, 22° 27' W; 1117 miles out; 1,255 mile to Oslo; day's run: 243 miles. It was getting light very early, about two in the morning, because we were so far north, and it was getting dark about 11:00 PM. We were not very far from the Arctic Circle. The wind came aft, and we put up the reacher. We were still moving along at ten knots. A couple of the depressions were coming toward us from the west.

The Fastnet Race was starting that day, but we wouldn't be there. It's a shame we missed it. We were only about three days late. We turned on the sauna and tried it out. The heat was wonderful. I dreamed I was back in Hawaii.

Day 6: Noon sight: 56° 59' N, 19° 40' W; 1,315 miles out; 1,057 miles to Oslo; day's run: 200 miles. The wind kept backing, and we jibed. We put up the 2.2 ounce super flanker spinnaker and the boat was stabler and quite a bit faster. We had "broached eggs," bacon, and blueberry muffins for breakfast. The barometer was dropping; the wind was building and coming forward. We took the chute down and put back up the reacher. The wind kept building and the barometer was diving. We were in for a real blow. We took the reacher down and put up the storm forestaysail, and reefed the main. The wind increased to thirty-five, then forty knots.

Day 7: Noon sight: 58° 12' N. 12° 57' W; 1,345 miles out; 827 miles to Oslo; day's run, 230 miles. We experienced a full gale during the night. It was really rough sailing; the wind was blowing steadily at forty-five knots with huge confused seas. But the morning weather map showed the depression passed to the north of us, and that the front had gone through.

The barometer slowly rose, which was a good sign. We shook the reef out of the main. The storm was gone, but heavy fog replaced it. We took down the staysail and put up the reacher.

Day 8: Noon sight: 58° 32' N, 5° 50''' W; 1,782 miles out; 590 miles to Oslo; day's run: 242 miles. Land Ho! We passed the Butt of Lewis, the northern point of the Outer Hebrides, at 9:30 AM GMT. It was a quick passage: seven days, twenty hours from St. John's to the Hebrides. We flew across The Minch to Scotland, reaching 16.5 knots on the waves with just the cruising reacher and mainsail up. We needed to reach the Pentland Firth between the Orkney Islands and the northern tip of Scotland before 8:00 PM GMT to not have the tide against us as we went through. The tidal current can run nine knots in the firth.

We just snuck through the firth before the tide changed. It was an absolutely beautiful passage, with green hills standing high above us dotted with old castles and little Scottish villages. It looked like something straight out of a storybook. But as soon as we got through the Firth, the rain started, and the wind died. It was our welcome to the North Sea.

The North Sea is very shallow, and I was expecting huge waves and icy cold winds. I have read horror stories about how nasty it can get, but we motored across a very calm North Sea, with oil rigs scattered around as far as we could see.

We motored through the night on calm, glassy seas, and sighted the coast of Norway in the morning. It was foggy, and we could only see a couple of miles. We passed a lot of ships, and small fishing boats and sailboats. We contacted the Royal Norwegian Yacht Club in Oslo. They were expecting us and had a berth ready. I think we were all ready for a hot shower and several lightning fast beers.

I stayed up most of the night navigating. When we entered the Oslo Fjord in the morning, it was very foggy. The visibility is only about one half mile. It's very tricky navigating up the fjord, because it is only about a mile wide, in parts, with unmarked rocks and shoals sticking out into the channel. We arrived at Oslo Harbor at 10:00 AM, and tied up at the Royal Oslo Yacht Club. After going through customs and immigration, we took a ferry across the harbor to Oslo, where we exchanged some money and bought some post cards and stamps. Oslo is a very clean and orderly little city.

I went for a run around Bygdoy, the area we were staying in. The King's Summer Palace is here, and much of the land is the King's farms. We took the day off and went sightseeing. I met a very nice Norwegian couple, Bjorn and Marit, and they took me on a tour of the city. We went to the Holmenkollen Olympic ski jump just outside of town and climbed to the top. The view was incredible! We then went to Frogner Park, which is filled with hundreds of statues by the famous Norwegian sculptor, Vigeland. The expressions on the figures were fantastic. Bjorn and Marit took me to their home, where I had a wonderful home-cooked Norwegian meal.

King Olav (with the cap) and Mr. Long on Ondine

We worked on the boat all day, preparing for the King, who was coming aboard the next day. We painted the deck, put any loose item away, and swept all the dirt under the rug. *Ondine* was a big attraction. Hundreds of people came by to look at the boat. The crew went out for dinner and a few drinks in Oslo. There were a lot of very drunk people walking around the city, and we were told by some locals that if you get caught driving with too much alcohol in your blood, you'll go to jail for three weeks, and you lose your license for two years.

It was a chaotic morning getting the boat ready for the royal party. We cleaned and polished everything in sight and dressed the ship. The club brought in a special ramp from the dock to the boat for the King to get aboard. He was 78 years old and didn't negotiate ladders very well.

The King and Crown Prince Harald arrived at about 4:00 PM. They were both very good sailors. Mr. Long had met King Olav while his shipping company was doing business with Norway, and they realized they both had a keen interest in sailing. King Olav won a Gold Medal in the 1932 Olympics in Los Angeles. Crown Prince Harald had won many European and world championships in his boats, all called *Fram*. Harald would be sailing with us on *Ondine* in the Maxi World Championships in Sardinia later in the summer.

I think all the important people in Oslo were around the *Ondine* that day. We went sailing with King Olav and Harald, and then Mr. Long threw a party for everyone at the Yacht Club. In the evening we had dinner at Peter Bosso's house up near the ski jump. It was a special evening. We swam in his pool, and used his sauna, then had a delicious barbecue followed by more than a few drinks.

When we tried to leave the Yacht Club in the morning, we couldn't get our anchor up. It was fouled around the chains holding the dock. Marty dove into the icy Oslo water, and untangled the mess, and we finally left Oslo at about 11:00 AM. The trip down the Oslo Fjord was spent securing all the loose gear we had aboard. The wind filled in from the south as we cleared the fjord and headed for the Skaggerak, between Norway and Denmark.

The wind blew all night at about thirty to thirty-five knots, with a short steep chop. It was pretty uncomfortable sailing, and several of the crew members were seasick—probably from drinking too much aquavit at the previous night's dinner. A lot of ships were passing by in both directions, and visibility was really poor with all the rain squalls. The barometer was dropping fast. It looked like we were in for some more bad weather.

It rained all night. The wind dropped and the seas flattened out, but were still confused. We were in the North Sea, just north of Denmark. There was a lot of shipping and the barometer was still falling. It was very dark and dreary. The wind clocked and filled in from the northwest until it was blowing gale force. Luckily it was aft of the beam, and we were flying along eleven knots, with just a reefed main and the staysail. We started to get some more leaks through the deck.

The next morning, the wind was still blowing hard, about twenty-five to thirty-five knots out of the northwest as we passed through clusters of oil rigs. Each cluster must have had thirty or forty rigs. It was like sailing through a city, with them all lit up. The wind came forward, and we put up the #3 genoa and full main and sailed hard on wind. It was really slow going; we had the current against us in the Strait of Dover, and we only made six miles in two hours. There were a lot of ships and ferries around; even some hovercraft going between Dover and Calais.

As we passed Brighton, then the Isle of Wight, the wind was on the nose, and cold. We were tempted to go into the Solent and take a look at all Whitbread Round the World Race boats getting ready to set off from Southampton. But the current was with us, and we didn't want to waste it, so we kept heading for Spain. There was a hurricane, Dennis, off the East Coast of the United States, and it was heading across the Atlantic. I hoped it wouldn't come our way.

As we crossed the Bay of Biscay, the sun came out, and it warmed up. It felt good to thaw out. The water temperature was 74 degrees, so we were back in the Gulf Stream. We were getting low on fuel, so we planned to put in at La Coruna, Spain, for diesel. We slowed down to save fuel, and also to allow us to get into La Coruna after daylight. There were a lot of ships passing by. It was like a freeway with a line of them to starboard heading south, and a line to port heading north.

The wind filled in from aft, so we put the 2.2 ounce chute up, and were doing 9.5 knots on a flat calm sea. It was sunny, and we were in T-shirts and shorts. We were going so fast, we decided not to stop at La Coruna. We would get fuel at Vigo, Spain, or Lisbon, Portugal.

The wind died in the morning, and we dropped sails, and started powering for Vigo, Spain, where we ran into a thick fog bank, and the visibility was reduced to about 100 feet. It was scary, because there were ships and fishing boats all around, and we could hear foghorns blowing from all sides, but we couldn't see them. We navigated our way into Vigo using the radar. The fog cleared up as we entered Vigo Harbor, and the fuel tank immediately ran dry. We switched to the second tank, and bled the fuel lines, and got the engine started again.

We tied up at the Real Club Nautico de Vigo. We must have been quite an attraction, because hundreds of people lined the dock to stare at us. It was a strange feeling, like we were monkeys in a cage. Once we cleared customs and immigration, we went into town and have a look around and grab a couple lightning fast beers.

We left Club Nautico in the morning and went to get fuel at the fishing dock. It was very foggy again, and navigating through the harbor was pretty tricky with all the fishing boats going in and out, the ferries crossing, and all the anchored ships.

Xargo, the Spanish maxi owned by the King of Spain, was at the fuel dock. It turned out that Vigo is *Xargo*'s homeport. We would be racing against them in Sardinia.

We left Vigo and headed out into pea-soup fog that stayed with us as we motored down the coast of Portugal. We put up the spinnaker for awhile, but the wind built, so we dropped to chute and put up the cruising reacher. We passed close by Lisbon, but couldn't see it through the fog.

We turned east, and entered the Strait of Gibraltar. We encountered a lot of traffic—twenty-two ships on the radar. The wind started to blow on our nose and the seas built up, coming out of the strait, so we tacked in close to the Spanish shore to get out of the wind and the seas. It was a slow trip through the strait with the wind, seas, and current all against us. We could see Tangier clearly on African shore.

We passed Gibraltar at about two in the morning, and we couldn't miss it, because it was all lit up like a bright building. Once we passed the rock, though, the wind and seas calmed down, and we motored into Puerto José Banús, arriving about 7:00 AM. It's a very modern resort and marina for the very rich. The customs man was classic. He wanted to know if the cowboys in the west of the United States still carried guns and had shootouts.

I went shopping with Sally at the supermercado in San Pedro de Alcantara. It was quite an experience. Huey wanted us to ask the manager for a discount, and I did. The manager told me that they didn't give discounts. I said we would have to go to another store, and he said they were the only supermercado in town. We ended up buying about seven shopping carts full of food, worth 67,000 pesetas, or about $650. The manager did give us a discount.

We went back to the harbor and were stowing the food, when we heard loud music. We went on deck, and who should be coming into the marina, but the old *Ondine*, that we had sold to the Brazilian navy. It was now called *Cisne Branco*, (White Swan), in Portuguese. And all the Brazilian navy cadets were aboard and dancing the samba, and the music was blaring as they came in and tied up next to us. Tom, Dave, and I went to lunch with the Brazilian crew. It was great fun catching up with them and to hear their sea stories.

As the sun went down, we left Puerto José Banús for Sardinia. We had seven new crew aboard, Mr. and Mrs. Long, Mr. and Mrs. Bosso from Oslo and their son Erland, and Alfredo and Graciela Iribarra from Buenos Aires. It was a beautiful calm evening of motoring across the Mediterranean under clear, starry skies.

The next day was hot and sunny, and Huey decided we should go into the island of Formentera and go for a swim. As we were going into the bay, we went aground. We hailed a small boat to give us a tow and were a bit shocked to see that all the passengers were totally naked. This is Europe! They took our line, and pulled, but we didn't budge. Several other boats came over and tried to help, but we were still hard aground.

Finally, we took a halyard and had one boat pull us over, while another boat pulled us astern. At the same time, we were powering full-astern with our engine, and we came free. We threw out the anchor, and went swimming. We dove down to check the keel, and found that a plate of aluminum had torn and was sticking out sideways. Dave went down with a hacksaw, and cut the plate off. We pulled up the anchor, and powered by Ibiza on an oily, calm sea.

It was still calm as we motored past Mallorca and Menorca. It was sunny, hot, and sweltering. There wasn't much to do except clean the boat, do some reading, and get as much rest as we could before the racing started. We needed to have the boat ready, so we could spend our days before the start in Sardinia practicing with the crew. Mr. Long was talking about taking the boat back the Palmer Johnson after the Maxi Worlds to have them fix it. I was hesitant because it was going to be hurricane season.

We sailed down the coast of Sardinia, and into Porto Cervo, picked up a buoy, and tied up Mediterranean-style (stern to the dock) at the Club Nautico.

Stuart Crust, my old Kiwi buddy from Tuia, was there sailing on *Xargo*. I gave him a tour of *Ondine*, and he gave me a tour of *Xargo*. We put our cruising gear into a locker, and cleaned the boat. I had a shower at the Yacht Club and a few lightning-fast beers with Stuart. We went to dinner at the local pizzeria, called the "Il Pomodoro" across the harbor. We hopped on the ferry back to the Yacht Club and noticed that the driver was not the real ferry driver, but a crewman off the Australian maxi, *Bumblebee*. There was a big ruckus; the police came, and we all got kicked off the ferry. It was a long walk around the harbor to the Yacht Club. But it was pretty funny. I got up early and went for a run. There were a lot of armed soldiers around town. With so much wealth in Sardinia, there is a big problem with kidnappings.

Sardinia is a funny place. It's like a movie set of an old, Italian village,

but the buildings are all brand-new. The Aga Khan, who owns Porto
Cervo, came aboard check out *Ondine*. Crown Prince Harald showed up
accompanied by a couple body guards. Harald would be racing with us,
and I wondered if the body guards would be, also. It was strange to see
him wearing a baggy pair of khakis and old golf shirt. He immediately
offered to help grind Charlie up the mast. I knew, then that Harald would
fit in fine.

Crown Prince Harald and John Jourdane

We went out for a practice sail and broke a running backstay, so we went back into the harbor to repair it, then motored to an island for lunch, and then went sailing again. My partner at the mast was Crown Prince Harald. It was pretty strange telling to a prince to do this and to do that. We would grind winches together, and I told him the best way to tail the halyards. I asked him what should I call him, your Highness? And he said, "No, call me Harald."

We packed all the sails, cleaned the boat, and basically got it ready to race. It was a royal morning. The Aga Khan, Baron Phillipe Rothschild, and King Juan Carlos of Spain all came aboard to tour the boat, and we went for sail.

The maxi *Condor* came in with her mast buckled in two places. It was a real shame; we were hoping to have some good racing against them. I think this was the densest concentration of big maxi racers and big boat sailors ever congregated in one place. Crown Prince Harald was now called "Harry" on the boat, and he loved it.

The first race was a disaster. We were late for the start but had a good first leg and caught up with *Kialoa, Xargo*, and *Bumblebee*. But we had lots of problems; we set a spinnaker in a classic hourglass, and had some very slow tacks. Our lack of practice was showing. But, we had some real talent aboard; Lowell North, Ben Mitchell, Dave Vietor, Jim Alsop, Cecil O'Malley, Mike Toppa, and Russell Long. We ended up in fifth place in the first race, behind *Kialoa, Xargo, Bumblebee*, and *Helisara*. The second race went well, and we finished third behind Xargo and Kialoa.

Woodii Carr, my old friend from Hawaii, came aboard for Race three and worked with Prince Harald and myself at the mast. It was a beautiful sunny day, with light air, and we finally had a good day of racing. The tactics and the crew work were great, and we finished in third place.

Ondine racing in Sardinia

Race four was the last race of the series. It was the offshore long-distance race—145 miles, from Porto Cervo, north to Corsica, then back to Porto Cervo. We had a good start in moderate air, and as the wind started building, we sailed inshore, out of the current, and tacked up the beach. *Xargo* ripped their mainsail and blew out their jib. *Kialoa* blew out their jib as well, and all of the sudden, we were leading the fleet. The wind died at sunset, and it was a long, frustrating night of drifting in little wind after we rounded the weather mark. We went through sail change after sail change. We finished third in the race, behind *Helisara* and *Kialoa*, and ended up third place for the series. It was *Ondine*'s first race series, and Mr. Long was quite happy.

The last day was match racing. This was probably the first time the big maxi boats had match raced anywhere. It was quite exciting. We raced *Kialoa*, and *Xargo* raced *Bumblebee*. The start was wild. We did about ten rapid circles in twenty-five knots of wind, and I thought the mast was going to come down. Ron Holland, the designer, was sailing with us today. Mike Toppa called our race tactics, and Harold Cudmore was tactician on *Kialoa*. Dennis Durgin was tactician on *Xargo*, and Gary Weisman was tactician on *Bumblebee*. *Kialoa* beat us, and *Xargo* beat *Bumblebee*, then *Kialoa* beat *Xargo* for the championship. It was great racing, and a lot of fun.

With the racing over, the crew started flying out, and we started loading on the cruising gear. Charlie and Eric left to fly home, and we moved the boat to the fuel dock and loaded up with diesel. I had a beer and said goodbye to Stuart Crust on *Xargo*, and we left Porto Cervo for Palma, Mallorca.

We motored all day on sunny, calm seas. We were all really tired. We had been going full blast for two months with very little rest. A crew of seven is just about the right size for delivering *Ondine*. We have three watches of two guys; three hours on and six hours off. Three hours is not too long on the deck, and six hours off gives you plenty of sleep.

Sally prepared a great lasagna dinner with fresh salad and Chianti, which we ate on deck under a full moon.

We sighted Mallorca in the morning and arrived at Palma about 3:30 PM. We cleaned the boat up and went to the marina pub for quick beer, where we met a bunch of friends of the crew. So we ended up having a few more beers, then went to Plaza Gomilla, and then to a disco at the Marina. Marty came home about 4:00 AM with three Spanish stewardesses, and woke me up to translate for him because they didn't speak English.

We cast off from the Club de Mar Marina, and headed for Gibraltar. We motored past Ibiza and Formentera, and were off Cartegena in the afternoon.

We arrived at Gibraltar about 11:00 PM and tied up in the old submarine pens, where we cleared immigration and customs. We got a few hours sleep and then started working on the boat cleaning, fixing, and buying provisions, fuel, and water. I went up the mast to take out a couple of halyards, and had a great view of Gibraltar Harbour. I went for my first run since Sardinia. I only ran about a mile, but it felt great. We went to the Barrelhouse Pub for beers, and the owner of the pub devised a light blue drink called an "Ondine." It is made of Parfait Amour, crème de menthe, and cream. The drink is the same color as *Ondine,* and it tastes awful!

The next day we went on a field trip up the rock of Gibraltar. We rode the cable car to the ape pits. There are a lot of Barbary apes living halfway up the rock. They are very tame, and come right up to you and climb on you, and they have evolved with no tails.

Approaching Gibraltar

Making a new acquaintance on Gibraltar

We went to the top of the rock, and looked over both sides, then walked through the old gun displacements and saw the huge water catchments on the Mediterranean side. We went to St. Michael's Cave, which is pretty impressive, and met up with Alan Coates of the Royal Signal Corps, whom we'd met the previous evening on the dock. Alan is a cave guide, and he offered to take us through the lower caves, which are not open to the public. It was a great adventure, just like something out of a Walt Disney movie. There were stalagmites and stalactites and curtains and columns and cave pearls. It is the only cave in the world besides one in Siberia with all ten types of cave formations. I'm still awestruck by the beauty of it. We spent three hours climbing through it on ropes and ladders and ledges. Then, as we were going back to the boat, there was an RAF flyby in celebration of "Battle of Britain Day."

We left Gibraltar early the next morning for Algiers. Dave, who is from New Zealand, and Phil, an Englishman, needed to get visas to get into the United States, and Algiers was the closest US consulate.

We arrived in Tanger, and were overwhelmed by guides and people wanting to help us. We hired Haji, and he helped us through customs, and then took us to the Kasbah, an ancient, walled, city market. We got quite lost wandering through the narrow alley ways. Haji assigned a boy named Mustafa to guard our boat. Mustafa was great. He showed Phil and me where to buy Moroccan wine, and where the American embassy was. He carried all our parcels, patiently waited while we went into stores, and he translated and bargained for us. We went to a rug factory, where they served us very strong mint tea, the local drink, and then bought Moroccan wine and saffron. Saffron was really cheap, about forty cents US for a half pound.

Sally and Mustafa in the Kasbah

Marty and I walked across town to a modern hotel on the beach, to go for a swim. As we walked along the streets, we were constantly accosted by young men asking to be our guide, or to sell us drugs. One guy kept saying, "Get high before you die," and "There's no hope without dope." We bought a couple of souvenirs, but no dope, and headed back to the boat.

We cast off, and headed for the Azores at 3:00 PM. Of course, the wind was right on the nose! It was a rough night. The shackle on the tack of the #3 genny broke, and the hydraulic system started leaking oil. We spent the morning fixing a broken bow pulpit and trying to find the leak in the hydraulic line.

As we approached the Azores, the wind died, and the seas flattened out. We were entering the Azores high, an area with little wind. We started motoring in light air and calm seas, then several rain squalls came through, and the wind was quite variable. We were in the "Horse Latitudes."

Happy birthday Marty and Tom! Marty and Tom were twenty-five and thirty, respectively, on the same day, and the wind was blowing twenty-five to thirty knots on the nose. We put up the #4, and reef in the already tiny mainsail. Our course was now taking us towards the Brazil. Sally baked a cake, and we had a birthday party for Tom and Marty.

The wind moderated some, and the seas lay down. It was a sunny day, and we went halyard flying. It's great fun. The boat looks fantastic while swinging from a halyard, twenty or thirty feet off the leeward side of the boat. Then the wind died to nothing; we had found the Azores High, and we started motoring.

We were faced with a difficult problem. We only had about three and a half days of fuel left, and Bermuda was about ten days away: should we power south to find the trade winds, power west, the shortest distance to Bermuda, or power north back into the storms? I voted for the first choice, because it was the warmer option.

The sea was very calm; just like in the North Pacific high. And there was a lot of junk floating around in the water also, but no Japanese glass balls. We saw a beautiful green flash at sunrise! A green flash is the phenomena of the last rays of the sun passing through the top layer of ocean, and produces a quick, brilliant flash of green. It is very rare to see one as the sun is coming up in the morning.

It was a clear and sunny day, so we stopped the boat and went for a swim. Everyone was in a good mood. We lowered the RPM's on the engine to conserve fuel, and headed straight for New York.

The wind filled in from the south. We put up the #3 and then the #4 and sailed through some pretty big squalls with lots of rain. There was a hurricane located at 25° S and 59° W. The wind died, and we powered on calm sea under sunny skies. Hurricane Irene looked like it would cross ahead of us, but hurricanes are pretty unpredictable. We were almost out of weather fax paper to boot. There was a big swell from the Northeast, and we motored all day. Phil made great tea in the afternoon. I was reading *The Great Gatsby*, and the tea fit in perfectly. Hurricane Irene was located at 32° north 55° west, about 450 miles away.

We passed the 10,000 mile mark on the log since leaving Sturgeon Bay in July. There we were, sitting in the cockpit watching the log turn 10,000 miles, when Bam! The cruising reacher blew out from luff to leech. We put up the #4. The wind kept building to thirty-five knots, so we took down the #4, put up the staysail, and put two reefs in the mainsail. The wind kept building to forty-five knots with huge seas; we were on the edge of Hurricane Irene. We took down the staysail, and were doing eight knots under deep-reefed main alone. Hurricane Irene was about 300 miles to the southwest of us.

October 1-Thursday-Day 10 out of Gibraltar, Noon site: 35° 18′ N, 39° 14′ W; 1,810 miles from Gibraltar; day's run: 148 miles. We had a very rough night. The wind was blowing forty-five knots, gusting to fifty knots, and there were thirty-foot seas. We tacked to the south to sail away from hurricane Irene.

I was putting on my gear to go on watch at 3:00 AM when there was a loud bang, followed by the boat standing upright, and a calming of the boat's motion. I ran on deck and found the mast had broken. It had snapped just above the upper spreaders, with the top fifteen feet of the mast hanging down. We cut free the head stay and back stay, and let them fall over board. Dave shimmied up the mast, cut the halyards and the mainsail, and lowered down the top fifteen feet of the mast to the deck. Then Kid went up and cut free the cap shrouds from the first spreaders, and we threw them over. We had a usable mast to the second spreaders. After about nine hours, we finally got the boat cleaned up enough to motor on course toward Saint-Pierre, the closest land, about 500 miles away.

Ondine's broken mast

The wind was about twelve knots and aft of the beam. We split the aft running backstays and led one set to the spinnaker sheet blocks, then we rigged the main halyard with the block on a strop around the mast at the second spreaders. We put up the storm trysail, and we were sailing again. The wind increased to about thirty knots with a lot of rain squalls. Several ships passed by, we were in a shipping lane.

The wind lightened and came aft, so we decided to put up more sail. We put another halyard on a strop over the second spreader, and set the

#5 jib and then set the staysail from the bow. It was a pretty good double-head rig, and we were sailing seven knots on course for Saint-Pierre. We sailed out of the Gulf Stream, and both the sea and air temperature dropped by 10°.

It was a cold, rainy, dark night. We took down the staysail and sailed with only the storm trysail. There was plenty of wind to keep us moving with just the trysail up. We set the staysail in the morning, and sailed until about noon under bright sunny skies. Then the wind died and a front moved in with dark skies and rain. We motored all afternoon, and were visited by a pod of porpoise and some whales. We passed the 100-miles-to-go point to Saint-Pierre, and we were getting very low on fuel. It was going to be close. Several rain squalls came through, but very little wind.

We did make it to Saint-Pierre, arriving at 6:00 AM. We tied up, and went through customs and immigration. We talked with Felix Park, who runs the local French language school. He let us use his phone to make calls. We worked on the mast, bought provisions, and did some laundry at Felix's house. He invited us to go to the public swimming pool with his students. It was great! We went back to the boat, had drinks with Felix and his wife, Jacqueline, and went to dinner at the hotel Ile de France.

I got up early and went for a short run, and did some shopping. We had lunch then cast off. Felix, Jacqueline, and some of the girls from the Language Institute came to say goodbye. It was a nasty, rainy day, with the wind blowing thirty-five knots. It was a reach and we were doing 10.5 knots with a little bit of mainsail and the staysail up.

The night was cold and rough. The wind blew forty knots, the air temperature was 40° F, and the cold rain and spray made it miserable. We passed through the Cabot Strait into the Gulf of St. Lawrence. It was still blowing forty knots, with rough seas and freezing spray.

My night watch apparel was as follows: sweat socks, thermal socks, wool socks, sea boots, underwear, long underwear, another pair of long underwear, wool pants, foul weather gear bottoms, long sleeve T-shirt, flannel shirt, wool sweater, down jacket, foul weather gear top, wool balaclava, wool gloves, wool mittens, and rubber mittens. It took me about twenty minutes to put on and take off my clothes.

The trees that were bright green when we came through here in July were now in full autumn colors: yellow, orange, and red. There was snow on hillsides as we passed by. Phil made a dodger for the helmsman using the floor board from the dinghy. Everyone laughed at it, but it kept the wind off, and we were all using it.

It didn't get above 46° F the whole day. We motored into the mouth of the St. Lawrence River, and passed towns with names like Trois Pistoles and Riviere du Renard. The going was very slow because the current was against us going up the river.

The boat was very cold below deck, because it was made of aluminum and had no insulation. Everyone was staying in their bunks or in the galley where Sally kept the oven going all the time.

There was a lot of current against us during the night. As the tide changed and ran against the current, the water became very rough. The seas were short, and steep, breaking over the bow of the boat with icy spray. We had a beautiful red sunrise with a full moon still up ("Red sky in morning, sailors take warning"). But it was so beautiful with the hills covered in brilliant orange, red, and yellow trees, we didn't think about the "warning." We motored past Quebec, and headed up the St. Lawrence River.

We motored into Montreal. The marina at Ile Saint Helene was closed for the winter. So we tied up at the commercial dock at the end of the Inner Harbor. We cleaned up the boat, went through immigration and customs, and went into town. A big part of Montreal is underground. There are shopping malls underground all over downtown.

We left Montreal in the morning, and started through the locks. This time we had to wait quite a while before entering each lock. There was a lot of traffic in the seaway; a lot of ships were going upstream. It was taking a lot longer to go up the St. Lawrence then it did coming down.

We finally cleared the last lock, Iroquois, at dawn, and motored through the Thousand Islands during the day this time. It was really beautiful with the trees showing their fall colors, we could see all the mansions and castles that dotted the shore. We passed into Lake Ontario.

We put the main up once more and sailed across the lake. The barometer was diving, meaning we were in for some heavy weather. The wind kept building as we approached the Welland Canal, and a gale warning was up when we arrived. We had to wait all night before we could enter Lock #1. A couple of ships had a problem passing each other, and jammed up the canal for many hours. The gale warning was changed to a storm warning. It was blowing fifty knots in the canal, so we decided to spend the day and night in Port Weller before we transited. We met a friendly sailor, Dick Nordstrom, who lived in Port Weller, and he offered us his car for the day so we could go visit Niagara Falls.

The next day it was still blowing pretty hard, but we went through the canal anyway. We were behind a really slow ore carrier, the *Algobay*, and it took us thirteen and a half hours to transit the locks. We had our first snow on deck as we arrived in Port Colborne on Lake Erie.

We left Port Colborne in the morning, and sailed into a very rough Lake Erie. It was blowing thirty-five to forty knots, and the lake is very shallow. The waters were just awful. They were eight to ten feet high, steep breaking waves, with the crests four seconds apart. We had one wave breaking over the bow and another still passing stern. The wind blew really hard all day. It was some of the worst sailing conditions I've ever been in.

The wind lightened up some, and clocked to the northeast, then built again. But at least it had come aft, and we were able to sail fast. We sailed up the Detroit River to the Detroit Yacht Club. It was very rainy and cold, but once at the club, we had hot showers and cold beers; a good combination.

It was another cold and rainy day. We took another hot shower and used the sauna before we left the Detroit Yacht Club.

The weather cleared up, and we had a starry night motoring across Lake Huron. The northern lights put on quite a show, with bright purple curtains covering the whole northern sky. The wind came up in the afternoon, right on the nose, of course, and it was filled with snow and sleet. It was really cold. The wind was on the nose almost all the way through the lakes, and when we changed course, the wind changed direction, so it was still right on the nose.

I have finally found the true meaning of cold. As we sailed through the Mackinaw Strait, the wind was blowing twenty-five knots on the nose, with snow and icy rain. The spray coming over the boat immediately turned ice, so the whole boat was covered with a layer of ice, including the helmsman. Icicles were hanging from the boom and the grinder pedestals. You couldn't walk on the deck; you had to slide over the ice on your butt. The lifelines were like a crystal lattice with eight inch icicles hanging down.

We crossed Lake Michigan in a gale that became a blizzard. This was a truly fitting ending for the voyage. We motored into Sturgeon Bay Canal and tried to take down the mainsail, but it was frozen into the mast, so Dave went up and pounded it with a hammer to break the ice. It finally came down, and we started motoring in to the Palmer Johnson Boatyard. Then we went aground. We put the boom out, climbed out on it in the snow storm, and finally got out of the mud. We motored into an empty slip at Palmer Johnson, and tied up the boat. We looked at the log, and found we'd gone 13,280 miles in the past six months. We had made it! We closed up the boat, and headed for the nearest warm bar. We could all feel a "Rum Squall" approaching.

Ondine was repaired at Palmer Johnson Boatyard that winter, and sailed south to Florida in February to race in the 1981 SORC.

Ten

Bahia Mar –

My Engine Nightmare

Forty-foot trawler – Fort Lauderdale to Curaçao

In January 1982, I received a phone call from Don Miller Yachts. Don himself, the man who recruited me to deliver Brian Keith's boat to Hawaii, asked me if I would be interested in delivering a new forty-foot trawler from Florida to the island of Curaçao. It would be an interesting trip, passing through the Bahamas, stopping in the Dominican Republic and Puerto Rico, and then heading south to Curaçao, an island of the Netherlands Antilles, off the northwest coast of Venezuela.

Being young and impetuous, I accepted the job without checking out the boat. After all it was a brand new boat that had been shipped from Taiwan to Florida and was "all set to go." I should have learned my lesson from Brian Keith's boat that new boats from Taiwan are not "all set to go."

I flew to Fort Lauderdale, Florida and met Don Miller. We motored down the New South River Canal, and went for a test run to Miami. The wind was out of the north at about fifteen knots, blowing against the Gulf Stream, so it was pretty rough, but we arrived at Miamarina about midnight with no problems.

The next morning my mate for the trip, Don Kreuter, arrived, and we loaded on the fuel, water, and provisions. I went to the customs office to clear the boat out of the United States, then went to take a last shower on land. Whom should I run into in the showers but Tom Corness, Dave Berridge, and several of my old mates from *Ondine*, who were in the marina preparing for the Key West Race. The sailing world is really small. A few beers and a lot of sea stories were called for, which of course we did. By the time we finally got into our bunks, we only got a couple hours sleep before leaving early in the morning.

At 1:00 AM, slightly hung-over and sleepy, we headed out of Miami for Nassau in Bahamas. The wind had picked up, and was now blowing twenty-five knots out of the north, against the stream. It was downright nasty, and we both had hangovers to boot. Crossing the Stream from Miami to the Bahamas is not an easy voyage, even in nice weather. The Gulf Stream is taking you north at five to six knots, so you have to set your course way south of your destination to get pushed up to it. And when the wind is blowing twenty-five knots against the Stream, the seas are very large, steep, and breaking. The boat was knocked around like cork in a washing machine.

As the day progressed, we started having trouble with the engines. One would stop, and I would have to bleed water and junk out of the fuel lines to get it started again. Then the other engine would stop, and I would have to bleed water and junk out of its lines and restart it. It got worse and worse, until I was bleeding fuel lines about every fifteen minutes. Both Don and I were getting tired, and decided to pull into the Bimini Islands to get some rest and work on the engines.

The sun was getting low in the sky, and we needed to get into the harbor before dark. It was an unbuoyed and unlighted channel winding through shallow sand banks. The sailing directions for entering Bimini Harbor read, "Head 080 toward the radio antenna, then when you see the ruins on the beach, head 060 between the breakers and follow the rocky shoal, then follow the darker twisting channel up the beach inside the breakers." We took a deep breath, crossed our fingers, and headed in. Somehow we made it safely to Weeches Dock, and went through Bahamian customs. We both got some much needed sleep. We would deal with the engines in the morning.

Bimini was a wonderful, quaint little island, with a population of only 200, and the town, consisting of the Hemingway Hotel, (where Hemingway used to stay and fish and write), a couple small restaurants, and a store. Everyone we met in Bimini, from Jerry, the dock master to Charles, the customs officer, to Lord Byron Bowlegs, the calypso singer at Opal's Fish House, was very friendly and helpful. I called Don Miller, and informed him of our problems, and he put me in touch with Ed, his head engine mechanic. We spent the day working on the engines, doing everything Ed said. I bled fuel lines, changed fuel filters, tightened fuel lines, and bled fuel lines, tightened fuel lines, over and over.

We left Bimini early the next morning, and made it about five miles, when both engines died again. We went back to Bimini and worked on the engines again. Then left in the afternoon, got about six miles, and they died again. So we motored back to Bimini. I called Ed, the mechanic, and he said to change the fuel filter gaskets, which I did. The engines died. He then said to unhook the hose from the fuel tank and stick it in a gallon of diesel. The engine ran fine until it used up the gallon. So the problem wasn't the engine, but the fuel. We had found the problem. The boat had been trial-run in Taiwan, then sat for a couple months in Taiwan, on the ship, and in Ft. Lauderdale. The fuel in the tanks had grown all sorts of living things that were clogging up the filters.

We had another problem. We were in Bimini with no way to clean our fuel tanks. So we did the next best thing—we emptied our fuel using a small twelve-volt transfer pump into fifty-five gallon drums, then put it back in slowly through a paper filter. It was a long and tedious job, but it had to be done.

Then, the next disaster occurred. I woke up the following morning feeling sick, and both my arms were covered with a bad rash. There was no one on Bimini to look at it, so I flew to Miami on the daily seaplane flight and went to Jackson Memorial Hospital. After waiting several hours in the emergency ward, I finally saw a doctor. He said I had a classic case of diesel poisoning. He said I should take antihistamines, rest for two to three days, and stay away from diesel fuel. I had to make a decision whether I should continue with the delivery or give it up.

I called Don Miller in New Jersey, and told him my situation. He said to rest, and he would take care of any medical bills. If I wanted to continue, he would send down Ed to go over the engines in Bimini.

I decided to continue and flew back to Bimini with Ed. We went through both engines top to bottom, and added an electric fuel pump, to make bleeding the engines easier. And by that evening were finally ready to head out. One positive that came out of the engine problems was that I got to know Bimini very well. We had spent a week on the cay, and were becoming "locals."

Our trip to Nassau was pretty uneventful. We only had to bleed the fuel line twice, and arrived safely in Hurricane Hole Marina. We felt like we had arrived in a different world than Bimini. Hundreds of boats, from small Bahamian conch boats to huge sailboats and power yachts populated the marina. This was the "big city" of the Bahamas, with trucks and buses and tourist resorts. There were even chandleries where we could buy whatever we needed for the boat. We spent the next day going over the engines and topping off the fuel tanks, then headed out for Allan's Cay.

The trip south to Allan's Cay was delightful. The sea was calm, the sky was blue, and the water was an incredible aqua color over the shallow sand banks. The anchorage at Allan's Cay was deserted, so we found a protected cove and anchored in fifteen feet of water. I dove in to check the anchor and was astonished by how clear the water was. I could clearly see objects 100 yards away in the water. After showering, Don and I sat on the fly bridge, and watched an incredible sunset. It was absolutely quiet except for the call of birds and chirping of the iguanas on the cay. The peace and beauty of the evening made the last week of engine problems fade into a distant memory.

The next morning, I got up early and swam to the cay. As I walked through the bushes, I noticed iguanas, lots of iguanas, and they were all coming toward me. They were like dogs, begging for food. Boaters who had been here before me had fed them, and they wanted food from me. It was kind of scary. I had visions of my bleached bones lying on Allan's Cay, and some fat iguanas greeting the next unknowing visitor. I quickly went back to the beach, and swam back to the boat.

We pulled up the anchor, and headed south along the Exumas, passing Highborne, Wax, and Staniel Cays. We anchored off Great Guana Cay to go over the engines, and have dinner. We went through Dotham Cut at sunset and headed down the Exuma Sound. The wind picked up and the seas started building. The fuel and gunk in the tanks started clogging the filters again, and the engine died. We were back to the changing filters and bleeding fuel lines again, but it was much easier with the electric fuel pumps.

I decided to change course. We headed into Georgetown on Great Exuma and worked on the fuel tanks again. We arrived at the entrance to the harbor at about 4:30 AM, and waited until dawn to head in. The sailing directions said it had "a tricky entrance with dangerous reefs." When it was light, we headed in. It wasn't that tricky, and we could easily see the reefs in the clear water. But it is better to be safe than sorry.

We tied up in the harbor by the keys and pumped the water, muck, and dirty fuel out of the fuel tanks with an electric fuel pump into some fifty-five-gallon drums. Then we moved the boat to the fuel dock at Georgetown, put in new fuel, filled the water tanks, and bought some supplies. We left the fuel dock and were headed across the harbor to the anchorage when the oil pressure alarm went off I shut down the starboard engine. We anchored, and I went over the engine. The whole starboard side of the engine room was covered with oil spray. We had broken a fitting where the oil line from the filter enters the engine block. I tried fixing it with Marine-Tex, but it didn't hold, so I connected two oil lines together with a fuel petcock as a connector and ran it straight into the block without the elbow. It seemed to work.

We went over the engines, changed the filters, and cleaned up the mess, then left Georgetown and headed south along Great Exuma to Hog Cay Cut. The engines died again, and when I checked the filters, they were full of gunk. Hog Cay Cut is very shallow, and we had to anchor and wait for high tide to get through. So, I worked on the engines, until the tide came in. Then we slowly worked our way through the cut. We went aground a few times, but eventually made it. We motored to the beach off Hog Cay, anchored, went for a swim, had dinner, and then got some sleep.

We woke at midnight. It was high tide, and we had a full moon, so we pulled up the anchor and headed for Long Island. We caught a nice red snapper while passing over the reef and had it for dinner.

In the evening we left and headed for Great Inagua. The weather was beautiful; we had a full moon and calm seas. The engines ran for about twelve hours without stopping, then they died again. We headed into Castle Island, south of Acklins Island, and anchored. We pumped out the fuel tank bottoms and cleaned the fuel filters once again.

We departed Castle Island and headed for Great Inagua, about eighty miles to the south. The engines ran fine for about eight hours, then died again. They weren't getting any fuel. I checked the tanks, and discovered the starboard one was dry I had closed the return valve and all of fuel had pumped into the port tank. We anchored at Man of War Bay on Great Inagua, and then in the morning we moved the boat down to the 200' x 200' dredged harbor at Matthew Town.

Tied up in Great Inagua

We went through customs and walked into Matthew Town to get some groceries and beer. Matthew Town is really "out island." It is very small, rustic, and the people are really friendly. Great Inagua is completely run by the Morton Salt Company. Most everyone on the island works for Morton, except for the drug smugglers. The island is also a major stop off for boats carrying drugs out of South America to the United States.

We were taking on fuel from a fuel truck, when a black Cadillac pulled up next to the boat. A couple very rough looking men got out of the car, and approached the boat. They asked to speak to the captain, and I went ashore. They wanted to know if I was there for a "pickup." I guess we looked like a drug boat. I told them no, we were just delivering the boat. Then they said they could fill the boat with marijuana for $50 a pound. We finished taking on fuel, cleared out of the Bahamas and headed for Puerto Plata in the Dominican Republic, 200 miles to the southeast, without any drugs.

The trip from Great Inagua to the Dominican Republic crosses the Windward Passage, and it was quite rough. The violent motion of the boat stirred up the fuel tanks, and we started having engine problems again. We did catch a nice twenty-pound tuna, though, and had a great breakfast of fresh tuna and scrambled eggs.

We made land fall at Monte Cristi, and motored up the coast to Puerto Plata. The windward side of the Dominican Republic is a beautiful mountainous coast with lush vegetation. It is quite a change from the low, palm-covered islands of the Bahamas.

We moored at the commercial dock in Puerto Plata and went through customs and immigration. We loaded on fuel and water, and hired two brothers, Francisco and Vinicio, to clean the boat, while I worked on the engines and generator.

Francisco and Vinicio took us into town for a local meal of rice, beans, platano, pollo, and beer. Then after the meal, they said we must go to the local brothel to see the "beautiful Dominican women." So, we went to the brothel and looked, but didn't touch. They were right, the Dominican women are beautiful.

The next morning was clear and sunny, and we motored along the Dominican coast on calm seas. The engines started acting up again, so we anchored behind Cabo Cabron in a beautiful cove (something out of a Tarzan movie), and worked on the engines.

We motored along the coast all day, bleeding the engines every few hours. We passed Cabo Engano in the evening, and headed across the infamous Mona Passage. It wasn't too bad, with only about fifteen knots of wind, and six foot seas. I had heard that this passage could get really nasty.

We motored slowly all night on just the starboard engine and passed Isla Despecho in the morning. The engine was dying about every two hours, but it was easy to prime, especially after putting the electric fuel pump in line.

We tied up Mayaguez, and went through customs and immigration. It's a dirty commercial port and has a very strong surge. So we left and motored to Puerto Real, a beautiful, calm anchorage among the mangroves.

We spent the night at Puerto Real, then left in the morning for Ponce. We tied up at the Ponce Yacht Club and enjoyed hot showers and a great meal.

I rented a car and drove to San Juan to get engine parts. It was a beautiful drive on the new "autopista" over the mountains. Puerto Rico is very similar to Hawaii. The temperature and vegetation are the same; only the language is different. And San Juan is just as crazy to drive in as Honolulu; the roads are jammed with cars going very fast, and there are one way streets that don't make sense to visitors.

Back on the boat, I pumped all the fuel out of the tanks, and put in new fuel, changed the fuel and oil filters, and changed the oil. I replaced the heat exchanger zincs, the air filters, and bled the engines.

We had a nice dinner at the Yacht Club; a fish called mero. It was delicious. It rained like crazy all night with a lot of wind. I got up a couple times during the night to check the mooring lines.

The morning was sunny and calm, and we headed out for Curaçao, some 450 miles to the south. The starboard engine was working fine, but the port one wouldn't start. The fuel line to the #6 injector was broken, so I replaced it, and the engine fired up. We finally had both engines working fine, and we were almost there!

We spent the next day cleaning the boat, putting up the Bimini top, making the boat ship shape for the new owner. It was my birthday, so we celebrated with rum and water and a fresh tuna dinner. We sighted the lumen of Curaçao after dark.

We arrived at Willamstad at dawn and tied up at the commercial wharf, where we went through customs and immigration. I called the new owner, and he said to motor the boat to the west end of the island to Piscadera Bay and tie her up at the Hilton Marina.

When we arrived at the Hilton, there was no place for us to put the boat, so we took her to the Curaçao Yacht Club in Spanish Haven. We scrubbed the boat, handed over the keys to the new owner, and had a couple well-earned beers.

Eleven

Brooke Ann and Crazy Horse

In 1982, I was approached by Larry Harvey to deliver his new Nelson/Marek 41, *Brooke Ann*, from San Pedro to Honolulu for the Pan Am Clipper Cup. As with all of Larry's boats, *Brooke Ann* was immaculate and well prepared. The trip to Hawaii was quick and comfortable, with no problems.

But Clipper Cup was a different story. The trade winds were very strong, and seas were huge. Many of the boats blew out sails, broke gear and masts, and a couple races were postponed because of too much wind.

The Molokai Race was especially bad. We had to beat across the notorious Molokai Channel, then up the North Shore of Molokai, cross the Pailolo Channel to Maui, round a buoy, then run back home to Diamond Head. The wind was blowing twenty-five to thirty-five knots with eighteen-foot seas. Needless to say, it was not a comfortable ride.

It was an overnight race, so Larry decided to treat the crew to a special meal of Chinese food. By the time we had crossed the channel to Molokai, greasy Chinese food and rice was scattered all over the inside of the boat. Moving around inside the boat was like skating on ice.

Overleaf: Brooke Ann in the Clipper Cup

We made it to Maui without breaking anything, rounded the buoy, and headed back down Molokai. The wind kept building, and the boat was sailing under spinnaker, barely in control. Then as we passed the old leper colony at Kalaupapa, the wind built to forty knots, and we started rounding up. First Bruce Nelson rounded up, and we gave him a bad time, then Larry rounded up, then I took over, and rounded up and wiped out. We rounded Ilio Point on the west end of Molokai, and the spinnaker wrapped around the head stay.

We couldn't get it down, so our French bow man, Phillipe, went up the fore stay in a bosun's chair to unwrap it, and he got wrapped up in the spinnaker. I can still remember him yelling, "Help, I am trapped, I am trapped." We finally got him down by sending up a knife, and cutting away the chute. When we finished the race, Phillipe ran off the boat and never returned. Even though the Molokai Race was a disaster, we ended up second in class for the series.

Antigua Race Week

Brooke Ann was sailed to Los Angeles, then put on a truck and shipped to St. Petersburg, Florida, to race in the Southern Ocean Racing Circuit (SORC). It was a series of races off St. Petersburg, around Key West to Ft. Lauderdale, triangle races to Bimini, Miami, and back, then the Miami to Nassau Race. We did well, ending up second in class.

Larry decided to race in the Antigua Race Week. So, I put a crew together, and we sailed the boat from Nassau to Puerto Rico to St. Thomas, U.S. Virgin Islands. We then sailed to Tortola, British Virgin Islands, where we were measured for the Caribbean Handicap used at Antigua Race Week. This was an interesting experience. The measurer measured the length and beam of the boat, asked us our draft and mast height, and measured the spinnaker pole. Then he went below and made a list of the interior furnishings.

Brooke Ann racing in Antigua

He came into the cockpit, sat down, and felt the deck. He said, "Oh gray deck, it gets very hot, we have to give you some rating advantage for your discomfort." It was quite a method of rating!

We sailed back to St. Thomas, where Larry joined us for a leisurely cruise to the Baths on Virgin Gorda and a pleasant stay at the Bitter End Yacht Club. We then sailed to Antigua, and pulled into Nelson Dockyard in English Harbour, where we stayed for the Race Week.

Lowell North sailed with us for the series, and I learned a lot. I felt like I was sailing with a legend. But at one point, I questioned his sanity. We were beating up north side of the island, and the wind had built from fifteen to twenty knots. Lowell asked if we could reef the #3 jib, and when we said no, he said, "give me a knife, and I'll make a hole in the luff so we can reef it." We declined, and ended up winning the race anyway. In fact we did well in most the races and ended up second in class for the week.

After the series was over, Stan Gibbs was driving a rental car and accidentally hit an Antiguan boy who was riding a motor scooter. The boy wasn't seriously hurt, but it was a big problem, because in Antigua, you are guilty until proven innocent. I went to the local constable's office and met Sergeant King, who was in charge of the island's police force. He said there was going to be an investigation, and we should hire a lawyer. Stan would probably go to jail, and the boat would be impounded until he was proven innocent.

So, that night, under the cover of darkness, we put Stan aboard, slipped out of harbor, and headed for St. Thomas. We stopped in St. Thomas and loaded on fuel and provisions, then headed out for Ft. Lauderdale.

All went well for the first couple days. Then about 500 miles out of St. Thomas, the rudder post snapped, and we lost all steering. We didn't have an emergency rudder, so we put out the spinnaker pole as a sweep, along with a bucket drogue, and slowly got the boat sailing again.

The closest island was San Salvador in the Bahamas, some 200 miles away. It took us three days to get there, but we made it. When we sailed into the bay at Cockburn Town, and when it looked shallow, we dropped the anchor. It went straight down, 150 feet and didn't touch bottom. The water was so clear, it looked 15 feet deep. We went in closer and dropped anchor again, and this time it stuck. I dove in to check the anchor, and was amazed. I could see clearly 100 yards in any direction, and the bottom was covered with a forest of bright colored corals and sponges.

We hailed a dive boat to tow us into the harbor, and tied up in a slip, then walked to the airport where we went through customs and immigration. I asked the Customs agent if there was anyone on the island who could build us a rudder. He thought about it, and then said we should see Marcus at his auto shop.

We went back to the boat, pulled out what was left of our stainless steel rudder post, and carried it into Cockburn Town. We wandered around a bit, checking out the monument to Christopher Columbus; this was where he first landed in the New World. I couldn't find an auto shop, so I asked someone, "where was Marcus's auto shop." And he said, "Marcus? He's probably at the Harlem Grill playing dominoes; it's over there around the corner."

We went to the Harlem Grill, and asked if Marcus was around, and a huge black man, came over and said, "I'm Marcus, what do you need?" I told him our predicament, and showed him our four feet of rudder post. He said, "Sit down and make me a blue print of what you want." I did it on a napkin from the Grill, and he said, "Come out back to the auto shop," which turned out to be a vacant lot with some broken down cars and an acetylene torch. He grabbed length of galvanized pipe out of a pile of metal, checked it for fit, and then cut it with a hacksaw. He inserted the rudder post in the pipe, drilled a couple holes and bolted them together. He then went to an old panel truck, and cut out a piece of the side with the acetylene torch. He welded the sheet metal panel, which still had a company logo on it, to the pipe. He picked it up and said "How's this?" I thought it was a little flimsy, so he cut some pieces of rebar, and welded them to the panel. It was perfect.

We drove the "new rudder" to the harbor in the trunk of his 1968 Chevy Impala, and stuck it in the boat. It fit and it worked! So, I asked him what we owed him, and he said, "Well, I hate to take advantage of you, but I need to feed my family, so it's going to cost you thirty-five dollars. It was probably the cheapest thing I had ever bought for a boat.

We left San Salvador and sailed the 400 miles to Fort Lauderdale. The rudder worked great. We arrived at the Derecktor-Gunnell Boatyard and hauled the boat out. Our boat sat there among million dollar yachts with our "Marcus Auto Shop rudder," still reading "the company logo."

Our San Salvador rudder.

When I told Larry Harvey the story, he said put the rudder on the truck hauling the boat back to California. He made it into a sculpture and put it in his back yard.

Crazy Horse

Larry commissioned Nelson/Marek to design him a bigger *Brooke Ann*. It was forty-nine feet in length and built by John Heinneman at High Tech Yachts in Noank, Connecticut. Stan Gibbs and I spent most of the winter 1983 in Noank watching over the construction. We trucked the boat to Florida for the 1984 SORC, and were doing great until the rudder broke. Mark Soverel of Soverel Yachts generously lent us a rudder off one of his boats, and we finished the series, doing okay. We knew the boat was very fast, if we could just keep a rudder in it.

Brooke Ann with her heat-shrink cover

I was to follow the truck hauling the boat across the country in the *Brooke Ann* van, and just before we left Fort Lauderdale, I was approached by man who worked for a plastic company. They had just developed a heat-shrink plastic to cover boats and cars for hauling. It would protect the boat from highway grime and flying debris. "It was going to revolutionize the boat hauling industry." He offered to shrink-wrap *Brooke Ann* for free, if he could use it in an advertisement. I said okay, it sounds good to me, and he proceeded to cover the boat with bright blue plastic.

The next day, the truck driver showed up, saw the boat, and said, "What the hell is that?" I said it was going to protect the boat; it's the newest thing." He replied, "Son, how many miles an hour is a hurricane?" I said seventy. Then he said, "This here boat is going through a hurricane for the next five days, and that cover ain't going to last 100 miles." I said, OK, but let's try it.

Larry Harvey on the new Brooke Ann

We left Fort Lauderdale, and before we reached Jacksonville, the plastic had blown off. The driver had been right.

The next summer we took *Brooke Ann* to Hawaii to race in the 1984 Kenwood Cup. We arrived early, prepared the boat, and had several days of crew practice. The day before the first race, we were out sailing in twenty to twenty-five knots of wind off Diamond Head, and snap! The rudder broke. We worked all night, built a new rudder, and made the start the next day.

During the Middle Distance Race, while beating up the North Shore of Molokai in thirty knots of wind, twenty-five foot seas, and a pitch black night, Rob Snyder went overboard during a tack.

Brooke Ann out of control in Hawaii

I was sure we would never find him in the conditions. But Bruce Nelson was steering, and thinking quickly, immediately crash-tacked the boat, and stopped it with backed sails. We actually backed down to Rob, and big Mike Howard reached over the transom, grabbed Rob, and pulled him aboard. Mike then said to Rob, "If you wanted to go swimming, you could have waited until we got back to the hotel."

We finished the series, and did OK, but the quickly built rudder wasn't right. I was getting very tired of breaking rudders.

I sailed the boat back to Los Angeles and had a good crossing. I like the return trips from Honolulu to the West Coast. They are relaxing and fun after the pressure of racing to and around Hawaii. We had been sailing for several days north to get into the high and had a fishing line out. Every day we had caught a mahimahi or two, but we couldn't get them aboard. As we got them near the transom, they would spit the hook and break free. Finally, after several days, we landed one, but as we got it into the cockpit, it spit the hook, and started flopping around the deck and toward the transom. I jumped on it, grabbed it, but it slipped out like a greased pig. Then another crewman jumped on it, and it slipped out. Then it flew down the navigators hatch into the navigation station, where a crate full of eggs was stored. It landed in the eggs, and started flinging raw egg and fish blood all over inside the boat, and this was in the tropics, where it all started rotting and smelling very quickly. It was not a pretty picture. But we finally had fresh fish for dinner.

When we got back to Los Angeles, Larry had decided that the *Brooke Ann* had had it with broken rudders, and that the boat had a "rudder curse" on it. So, his answer was to change the name. He renamed the boat *Crazy Horse*, and not only did it stop the rudder losses, but the boat started winning every race.

We went back to Hawaii in 1986, and raced the Kenwood Cup; Larry took no chances, we checked and double-checked everything, and had both Bruce Nelson and Paul Cayard sail with us. We ended up first place overall and won the Kenwood Trophy.

Twelve

NZI Enterprise
Whitbread Round the World Race
1985/86

Skipper—Digby Taylor
Crew—Murray Ross, Mike Keeton, Ross Field, John Jourdane, Graham Fleury,
Greg Blomfield, Mark Hauser, Matthew Smith, Jeremy Scantlebury, Steve Wilson,
Ken Davies, Phil Harris, Grant Jenkins, Kendal Law, Graeme Kendall

I was all set to navigate the Frers 50 *Tomahawk* in the 1985 Transpac
Race, when I received a phone call from Digby Taylor, the skipper of
Enterprise New Zealand. They were 300 miles from Panama, delivering the
boat to England to race in the 1985 Whitbread Round the World Race and
their navigator had decided to leave. They needed a navigator for the
Whitbread, and he wondered if I was interested. I said, yes, of course I was
interested. The Whitbread was the "Mount Everest" of yacht racing, and
I had always dreamed of doing it.

Digby asked me if I could be in Panama in three days to help deliver
the boat to Portsmouth, England. If I worked out on the delivery, then
I had a spot on the Whitbread Race. I said I would see him in Balboa,
Panama, in three days. Then I had to call John Arens, the owner of
Tomahawk, and tell him I couldn't navigate the boat in the Transpac

Race, which also started in three days. I felt bad leaving at such short notice, but John was very gracious, and said he understood, and that he would do the same thing if he had the opportunity.

I arrived at the Balboa Yacht Club, and joined the *Enterprise* crew. We had to have the boat measured to transit the canal, and that, along with all the paper work, took four days. We finally did pass through the locks with a small ship, and made it across Lake Gatun and to San Cristobal on the Atlantic side in one day. San Cristobal is a notoriously rough town, with lots of drug trafficking, and crimes of all sorts. There was a sign at the San Cristobal Yacht Club that said, "One dollar for a taxi may save your life."

We cleared customs and headed north towards the United States. The area off Nicaragua is dotted with small islands and coral reefs. Our course took us in a northwesterly direction, which would take us close to the Rocador Bank. The trade winds were blowing, and the sea was getting fairly rough. I went below to get some sleep. I was awakened by a crewman who said they had the Rocador light in sight, but the sea had suddenly calmed. I told myself, "Uh oh," and at that moment there was a huge crash, and I thought, "We've lost the mast." The guys on deck said nothing had broken, but thought we had hit something. We dropped the jib and slowed the boat down, and started to get a fix using the bearing of the light and the depth sounder.

Five minutes later there was another crash. This one was for real; we were hard aground on a coral reef off Nicaragua, which was at war, and allowed no outside ships or yachts in its territorial waters. We all imagined a Nicaraguan navy ship pulling up, arresting us, and taking us to a dank and dirty prison on the mainland.

Right: The Bruce Farr-designed 80 foot NZI Enterprise

NZI Enterprise traversing the Panama Canal

We tried leaning the boat over in the hope we could work our way off the coral into deeper water, but it didn't work. We tried for several hours, with everyone looking for the best way to get off; no recriminations or arguments, just a team of guys working together. But we finally had to face it; we were stuck. So we took down the mainsail, and threw out a couple anchors, and waited for the morning light to see our predicament.

When morning came, we saw we had just hit the atoll on the west corner, and we were able to use an anchor and the engine to pull us clear. Once in deep water, we pulled up the entire floorboard and checked for leaks, and Graham Fleury dove over with a mask to check for damage. He said there were a couple cracks in the fairing and the lead torpedo at the bottom of the keel was a bit gouged, nothing looked serious.

We headed towards Florida, where we decided to haul out at the

Derecktor-Gunnell Boatyard in Fort Lauderdale to check the hull and keel. It turned out, that we had only bent some of the lead on the keel bulb, and we were able to pound it back in place with a sledge hammer.

After a couple days rest in warm, bikini-clad Fort Lauderdale, we headed off up the East Coast. We were sailing in the Gulf Stream, and the current gave us an extra three to four knots of boat speed, and we made the passage quickly. When we reached the Grand Banks off Newfoundland, the fog settled in, and we couldn't see the bow of the boat. We had a spinnaker up, and were sailing fast. We could see targets of fishing boats on the radar, and they were all around us, but we couldn't see them. We were doing thirteen knots and all of the sudden, we hit something and the boat stopped. I ran on deck, looked over the side, and saw a huge whale swim out from under the boat. We must have hurt him, but he just leisurely swam away. We took the spinnaker down, and decided to sail slowly until we were out of the fog.

Once we cleared the Grand Banks, we had a quick run to England in strong winds and following seas. At one point we covered 1,000 miles in 3 days. This was a distance that was in excess of anything that had been achieved in previous Whitbread Races.

We arrived in Portsmouth, and moored the boat at Camper & Nicholson's Marina in Gosport. The crew was put up in rooms at a local college, and we started preparing the boat for the start of the Race. Our riggers, Steve Wilson, Matthew Smith, and Grant Jenkins, pulled out the mast and x-rayed it for any cracks. Murray Ross and Mark Hauser went over all the sails. Mike Keeton took charge of going through the whole boat, and organizing everything. Ken Davies, Phil Harris, and Graham Fleury went through all the winches, tearing them down and lubing each one.

Ross Field and Jeremy Scantlebury worked on the hull and deck, reinforcing the backstay mounting and improving the mainsail track. Greg Blomfield went through all the deck gear. I went through the navigation station, trying to improve the reliability of all the components.

Digby is a do-it-yourself, pull-yourself-up-by-the-bootstraps kind of Kiwi. So when we hauled the boat out at Moody's boatyard in the Hamble, he decided to paint the bottom himself, to save money. We covered the boat with ground-length plastic to keep the toxic bottom paint from getting on other boats and humans. The paint was Micron 22, a very toxic paint containing cyanide. I told Digby he should have the boat yard spray it, but he said, "No problems, mate, it's easy." He proceeded to put on a dust mask and start spraying under the tarp bare-chested, wearing only shorts and topsiders. I was aghast, and then to top it off, when he finished spraying, he washed himself down with acetone!

Leg One – Portsmouth to Cape Town

The start was a mad house. Thousands of spectator boats cluttered the Solent to watch the twelve race boats leave. There was a layer of fog, so it was difficult to see the other boats as we jockeyed for position on the starting line. But somehow we made it without a collision and headed down the Solent and out through the Needles under spinnaker at good speed.

We worked the boat hard all night, and as we passed Illes d'Oessant, on the corner of France, we were in first place. As we sailed across the Bay of Biscay, heading for Spain, all the maxi yachts were very close to each other. We could use the radar to plot the positions of the other boats.

The Bay of Biscay can have horrendous weather, but we were let off easy, with ten knots of wind from the southeast. We couldn't ask for better conditions to start a 7,000-mile trip.

We rounded the southern headland of the Bay of Biscay, Cape Finesterre, still sailing in moderate wind from the southeast. A major strategic decision had to be made at this point. The choice was whether to sail hard on the wind directly down the coast on a course that would take us a little closer to Cape Town at a slower speed, or whether to ease sheets a bit, and sail away from the coast at a higher-speed, but with more distance. We did a lot of calculations and came to the conclusion that it would be better to sail freer and faster.

We sailed close to *Drum*, from England, and *Portatan*, from South Africa, for several days before reaching the latitude of the Canary Islands. As we approached the Canaries we sighted *Portatan* about three miles behind us. *UBS Switzerland* and *Lion New Zealand* were both well out to the west of us, and had decided to sail freer and faster than we were.

The next day we sighted the Canary Islands and sailed between them and the mainland of Africa on our course towards the Doldrums. The position report given after we cleared the Canaries gave *UBS* a lead on us of 120 miles. *Lion New Zealand* was 90 miles ahead, and we were leading *Portatan* by 150 miles. *Drum* was thirty miles behind *Portatan*, with *Cote d'Or*, from Belgium, another fifty miles behind them.

Sailing down the coast towards the Cape Verde Islands, which are just north of the Doldrums, we picked up the Portuguese trade winds, and began to clock big daily mileages in the twenty-five to thirty-five knot northeasterly wind almost directly behind us.

Several days after leaving the Canaries we went on a jibe that took us away from land. We stayed on this jibe a little too long, but we felt it would possibly pay off for us later, as we approached the Doldrums. It is generally considered to be more advantageous to go through the Doldrums well to the west. While on this course we came across *Lion*, which had decided to come in toward shore.

UBS Switzerland sailed ahead of us into the Doldrums, at what looked the best place to go through. But they stopped right there, seemingly unable to move. Each day as we approached the Doldrums, we caught up with *UBS* and put time on *Lion* and the rest of the fleet.

We went into the Doldrums just fifty miles west of *UBS*. We came out of the Doldrums three to four days later with the *UBS* was a comfortable sixty miles behind us. *Lion New Zealand* fifty miles back, and *Drum* was eighty miles back. *Portatan* decided to take the amazing option of continuing to sail into the Doldrums close to the coast, where there should have been no wind.

Then came the real tactical puzzle of the South Atlantic. As you sail out of the Doldrums, the wind is coming from the south southeast while the course to Cape Town is southeast. So, you have to sail either east into the coast of Africa, or South, not toward Cape Town.

Ten days out from Cape Town, *Lion New Zealand* caught up with us, and we came in sight of each other. But it took us just twelve hours to put them on the horizon behind us. We definitely seemed to be faster in these conditions. But we would pass each other many times.

In the meantime *Portatan* and *Cote d'Or*, contrary to the Pilot Chart, did not find less wind to the East, and were well ahead of us. This meant that they were now first and second in the race, *UBS* was third, *Lion* and ourselves next, and then *Drum*.

The wind started to freshen and we began to sail in strong trade winds that were much more to our liking. In the process of putting a reef in the main, the main halyard broke, and the sail flogged and disintegrated. We removed the sail, and hoisted the spare main. That little episode caused us to slow down for a period of about ten hours, and *Lion* passed us again.

The breeze continued to build to gale proportions, and all the Maxis had to power hard on the wind towards Cape Town. Sailing conditions were rough, although the wind was not fierce, maybe thirty-five to forty knots, the seas were large and very steep. We had to slow the boat down to six or seven knots, so we wouldn't fly off the twenty-foot seas, and crash into the bottom of the troughs.

NZI pounding to weather toward Cape Town, South Africa

The next day we heard on the radio *Cote d'Or* had started to delaminate in her bow. Her hull was breaking down, and she was going to head for Luderitz, a little port on the west coast of South Africa, some 800 miles north of Cape Town. We heard nothing from *Portatan*, and in the meantime we had passed *Lion New Zealand* again.

Just after this report, I heard a shout from the deck, "the mast has gone!" I rushed up on deck and to my amazement, the mast was still standing, but with an enormous kink in it about three quarters the way up. The top section of the mast was bent at an angle of 35° to vertical. This presented a real problem. The running backstays that support the mast when the boat is running downwind were attached above the kink. Our only option was to reduce sail, by reefing the main, put up a storm jib, sail more on a reach, to unload the mast, and then try to strengthen the mast at the kink.

In the meantime *Drum* had also begun to suffer hull damage from the constant pounding in the huge, steep seas, and like *Cote d'Or*, the crew was sailing for Luderitz. We hadn't heard from *Portatan* for forty-eight hours, and we began to wonder if they had suffered some failures as well.

At daybreak the next morning our mast was, thank goodness, still standing. We erected some temporary backstays in the rigging to hold the mast up while we ran downwind, and attempted straighten it, For the next twelve hours there was someone up the mast practically all the time, trying out one idea or another to save the mast. Eventually we did manage to partially straighten it, and were able to sail reasonably well towards Cape Town. Since the mast was bent to starboard, we were able to sail on starboard tack OK. But on port tack, however, when the bend in the mast was on the wrong side, we had to reduce the load. So, each time we tacked, we either had to add on sail or reduce sail. It meant a lot of work for the crew. Needless to say, we didn't tack more than we had to.

We finally heard from *Portatan*, and they were leading by more than 100 miles when they lost their mast, and headed for Luderitz to make up a jury rig in the hope of at least finishing.

We continued sailing towards Cape Town at the best speed we could achieve. *UBS* finished first, sixteen hours ahead of *Lion*. We finished ten hours later.

South Africa

We spent the first week in Cape Town cleaning the boat fixing the broken gear working on the mast and getting everything in order.

We moved off the boat into some apartments not far from the Royal Cape Yacht Club. This was during the time of apartheid, and an interesting situation developed.

The Whitbread fleet in Cape Town

The Royal Cape Yacht Club did not allow blacks to enter, but one of the crewmen on the Dutch boat, *Phillips Innovator*, was a black Dutchman. So theoretically, he could not enter or leave the yacht club. To resolve the problem, the club made him an honorary white, and gave him a yacht club membership card that said "Honorary White."

The crew of *NZI* all got a week off for vacation, and I took off to see the wild animal game parks in northwest South Africa. I flew to Johannesburg and rented a car and drove to Sabi Sabi Game Park. It was an incredible adventure. I slept in a native boma and was given a personal guide.

Each day we would go out, either in a Land Rover or on foot, sightseeing and taking photos of the wild animals. I saw elephants, rhinos, giraffe, gazelle, African wild dogs, warthogs, and leopard. It was an adventure I will never forget.

On safari with my guide, Ian, at Sabi Sabi Game Park

Rhinoceros at Sabi Sabi Game Park

Leg Two – Cape Town to Auckland

The start was quite different than in England. It was bright and sunny, there were few spectator boats, and the wind was light and variable. We sailed along the shore toward the Cape of Good Hope, the southern-most tip of Africa, and the wind slowly built until it was blowing fifteen knots at the Cape.

The maxis all stayed pretty close for the first few days. On the fourth day, the wind filled in from the northeast at twenty-five knots, and we took off at fourteen knots of boat speed. We were in first place, with *UBS* in second, and *Atlantic Privateer* (new name for *Portatan*) in third. Then, *Privateer* dove south, and found more wind, and moved into first place. We were in third.

The weather maps were beginning to look like mine fields, with up to a dozen low pressure systems on a single map. It was very important that we stay north of the lows, where the wind was from behind, If we sailed south of the low, we would have strong winds on our nose, which was not only uncomfortable, but would not allow us to sail toward New Zealand.

In this mess, the maxis began to duck and dive all over the ocean, trying to position themselves for the next incoming low.

Friday, December 13 was a day we won't forget. We were sailing under spinnaker in thirty to thirty-five knots of wind when we broached, and the spinnaker pole broke. We put up our spare pole, but the after guy kept coming out of the end fitting. Then the fore guy broke, the pole skied, and the boat became very unstable. Then the inboard end of the pole came off the mast. And to top it off, during all this, the broken spinnaker pole rolled off the deck into the water. Now we only had one pole for the rest of the leg.

High speed sailing in the Southern Ocean

We finally got everything settled down, and took off surfing toward New Zealand, and two days later we were back in the lead. And by the time we passed Heard Island, we were sixty-five miles ahead of the next boat, *Atlantic Privateer*.

We sighted our first iceberg, and everyone's heart started beating a little faster. We started keeping an iceberg and growler watch.

Icebergs are big and easily seen visually or on radar, but growlers, are broken-off pieces, that float just on or below the surface, and could open us up like a can if we hit one.

The only bathing facilities on *NZI* were cold water showers. The water was taken directly from the sea, and pumped aboard. Mike Keeton showed how tough he was by taking a shower at 55° south latitude in water that was one degree above freezing. Everyone decided he was totally mad.

How cold was it? There were some spare jib sheets on the deck, and they were frozen solid. So, we put them below deck, and three days later, they were still frozen solid.

On December 22, we received a storm warning from Perth radio, saying, "Expect very rough seas with heavy swells and wind 55 to 60 knots." We all had a sinking feeling in our guts. The crew went through the boat, lashing everything down and preparing the storm sails. David West, the cook, made sure everyone was well fed and made up sandwiches and hot drinks, as there would be no cooking for the next couple days.

The wind came in strong and on the nose. It was tough going, but we made it through with no damage. And as if it were a Christmas present, the wind and seas abated for Christmas Day. We had a dinner of turkey, plum pudding, and champagne.

As we approached Cape Reinga in New Zealand, Atlantic Privateer, was seven miles ahead of us, in the lead. We worked the boat hard, and by the time we passed the cape, we were within a half mile of Privateer. We rounded North Cape dead even. We raced boat for boat down the East Coast toward Auckland. Crowds of boats jammed with spectators came out and cheered us on. Atlantic Privateer sailed just enough faster to beat us in, by just 500 yards. Not a lot, after just sailing 7,000 miles!

The moment we crossed the finish line, we relaxed and looked around at the hundreds of spectator boats. Sailing up the Inner Harbor to Marsden Wharf, we congratulated Atlantic Privateer. Then we waited while they motored into the dock, where there were fifteen to twenty thousand people waving and cheering.

Arrival in Auckland, Atlantic Privateer and NZI

New Zealand

We spent a week cleaning and fixing the boat. We pulled the masts and hauled the boat to paint the bottom. I started learning about "Kiwi hospitality" when Lin and Coleen Carmichael, whom I had met at the Clipper Cups in Hawaii, insisted I move out of my hotel and into their house. They treated me like a son, and made me a part of their family.

Just before we arrived in New Zealand, the Greenpeace ship, *Rainbow Warrior*, had been mined and sunk in Auckland Harbor by French military. The Kiwis hated the French for that. There was a French boat in the race. *L' Esprit d' Equipe*, and they had broken their steering on Leg Two.

There was a rule on *NZI*, if you clog up the toilet, it is your responsibility to take it apart and unclog it. When we arrived in Auckland, the toilet was clogged, and no one would take responsibility to fix it. So, the day after our arrival, I was in the head in the back of the boat fixing the toilet, when two crewmen from *L'Esprit d'Equipe*, came aboard and asked if they could take some pictures of our steering system to use in designing a new one for their boat. I said," yes, crawl back behind the toilet and take all the pictures you want." Meanwhile, I was putting the hoses to the toilet back together, and pumping the system. I pumped and pumped, and all of the sudden, there was an explosion behind the head, and the two French crewmen came running out screaming and covered with *NZI* feces. All the Kiwis on the boat and dock started clapping. They all thought I did it on purpose. I was a hero.

John Jourdane in the "high tech navigatorium" on NZI

When the boat was back in the water and at Marsden Wharf, we had an open house to show the New Zealanders their boat. I was in the navigation station explaining what all the instruments did. Quite often, the visitors would say, "you're not a Kiwi, what are you doing on this boat?" I would explain that I was a navigator, and Digby asked me to sail with a boat load of Kiwis." Then the visitor would say, "Have you seen our country?" I would say no, but I plan to visit the South Island next week. Then they would say, "You must call my brother, or uncle, or mother." So, by the end of the tour, I had a stack of numbers to call.

I went to the South Island, and visited Christchurch, Queenstown, and hiked the beautiful the Milford Track, where I met Steve Lind and Roger and Linda Blackburn, who have become lifelong friends. Then, just for the fun of it I called one of the numbers I had been given on the tour of *NZI*, just to say hi. When they heard who I was, they said, "Mate, we've been waiting for your call, your room is ready." Now, that is hospitality!

Roger, Steve, Linda, and John on the Milford Track

Back in Auckland, we started provisioning the boat, and getting ready to leave on Leg Three. I made the mistake of going out for a "few beers" at the Leopard Tavern with the South Africans off *Atlantic Privateer*. When I ordered a pint and they each ordered their own pitcher, I knew I was in over my head. Then after several pitchers, one of them yelled, "Chunder Test!" Then they went across the street to the park, and proceeded to see who could vomit the farthest. After they finished, they went back in and ordered more pitchers. These were rough guys.

Leg Three—Auckland to Uruguay

The start in Auckland was in light air amongst thousands of spectator boats. We had a spectator boat get in our way just as we were approaching the line, and had to jibe away. So, we were about thirty seconds late getting to the line and in dirty air from the other maxis.

Rounding Coromandel Peninsula at dusk, we were in fourth place. Thirty miles later, going past Cuvier Island, we passed *Lion*, and settled down to catch *UBS* and *Cote d'Or*. At daybreak the next morning, we were even with *Cote d'Or* and *UBS* as we set a course for the Chatham Islands.

When we reached the Chatham Islands, we had taken over first place. The wind filled in, and we were moving along nicely heading south to get to the "Roaring Forties." A couple days later, we were sailing under a full main and blast reacher, doing thirteen to fourteen knots of boat speed, when there was a crash and then quiet, then all hell broke loose. Someone yelled down, "The mast has gone, all hands!" We ran on deck to see the mast broken in two places, and the sails hanging over the side of the boat. Hardly a word was spoken. Everyone was stunned.

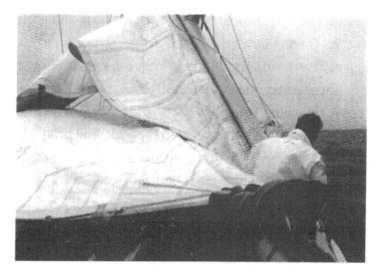

NZI Enterprise's crumpled mast.

In shock, almost silently, we set about getting the mast sections back on board. There was a danger of that the mast could puncture the hull. Then we set about erecting a jury rig. We managed to get some staysails up sideways on the stump of mast left, and we started sailing back to the Chatham Islands. Our race was over!

NZI in the Chatham Islands

Thirteen

Pat Farrah–
Ragtime and Blondie

When I returned from the 1985/86 Whitbread Race, Pat Farrah hired me to run his two boats, *Ragtime*, a 61-foot Spencer design, and *Blondie*, a Santa Cruz 70. Pat was a great boat owner. Everything he did was done first class; the best boats, the best equipment, the best crews, the best accommodations, and the best parties. Pat liked to have fun sailing and that meant everyone on his boats and the other boats to have fun also. He was a gentleman first, an avid racer second, and great party host.

We raced *Ragtime* from Los Angeles to Hawaii in the 1987 Transpac Race, and he loaned *Blondie* to his friend Bob McNulty. Neither boat won, but we had the best parties. Pat rented Coconut Island in Kaneohe Bay, and took the two boats; their crews, family, friends, and anyone else who wanted to go. It was a wild day with barbeque, dinghy races, volleyball games, and dancing.

Pat left *Ragtime* in Hawaii, and I delivered *Blondie* back to Long Beach. We raced *Blondie* in the West Coast races and *Ragtime* in the Hawaii races. It was a busy time. I would fly to Honolulu to look after *Ragtime* for a couple weeks, and then fly to Long Beach to look after *Blondie* for a couple weeks.

Pat Farrah steering Blondie

Eventually it became too burdensome to commute back and forth, and Pat hired a very able sailor in Honolulu, Ty Prine, to look after *Ragtime*. Ty did a great job, and continued looking after the boat until Pat sold her.

Racing on *Blondie* was special. We were very successful, because Pat always put together the best crews. I had the honor of sailing with some of the best racing sailors on the West Coast.

Pat loved to race *Blondie* to Mexico, especially to Manzanillo, where we stayed at the Las Hadas Resort. Pat always rented the Presidential Suite with its huge courtyard. Then he would announce the "Bikini Ping Pong Tournament." Then he would invite all the women on all the boats, and all the guests in the hotel to participate. The winning prize was one million pesos! It sounds like a lot, but when converted to dollars, it was only about one thousand U.S. dollars.

The courtyard would be turned into a fabulous fiesta. He would have a ping pong table set up, and a catered buffet of lobster, shrimp, ceviche, tacos, and so on. Of course there was a full bar with unlimited margaritas, beer, and sodas. It was a wild party. Everyone had a great time, but probably no one more than Pat. His Bikini Ping Pong Tournament was one of the highlights of the Manzanillo Race.

When Pat bought *Blondie* in Hawaii, they threw in a cigarette-type powerboat, called the *Excalibur Hawk*. So taking care of Pat's "fleet," I inherited the *Hawk*. It was very fast, but a pain in the butt. The engines were highly tuned, and always breaking down.

Pat would call me early Sunday morning, and say, "go warm up the engines on the *Hawk*." And I would go down to the slip in front of his house on Alamitos Bay and start up the engines. Then Pat and a couple friends would show up, and we would leave the dock about 7:30 AM. We would fly across the water at high speed to Avalon on Catalina Island, walk up into Avalon to the Marlin Bar. Pat would wake the owner, who would open the bar. He would throw down a couple hundred dollar bills, and say, "rum and cokes all around." Then we would walk out on the pier and get buffalo burgers at Ricks. We would hop back in the *Hawk*, fly across the water back to Long Beach, and tie the boat up in Pat's slip. It would only be 10 AM!

Fourteen

Fisher & Paykel, New Zealand
1989-90 Whitbread Round the World Race

Fisher & Paykel, New Zealand—Farr 82-foot ketch
Skipper—Grant Dalton
Crew—Murray Ross, John Jourdane, Keith Chapman, Andrew Taylor,
Grant Spanhake, Ken Davies, Shaun Connolly, Eric Dewey, Ross Halcrow,
Matthew Smith, Jeff Scott, Tom Warren, Alec Rhys, Steve Trevurza, Ed Danby

I had just helped deliver the Whitbread maxi, *The Card*, from England to Majorca, Spain, when I received a phone call from Grant Dalton in Australia. He said they had just sailed their new Farr 82 maxi ketch, *Fisher & Paykel*, from New Zealand to Australia and were losing their navigator. Was I interested in trying out for the position for the upcoming Whitbread Race?

I said yes, and hopped on a plane to Australia. It wasn't an easy flight. I flew from Majorca to Madrid to London to Pittsburgh to Los Angeles to Honolulu to Auckland to Sydney to Brisbane. It took thirty-six hours, and I arrived more than a bit dazed. It was great for sailing though, my body didn't know what time zone it was in, and I eased right into the watch system.

Opposite: Fisher & Paykel sailing in New Zealand

We sailed the boat from Brisbane, across the Tasman Sea to Auckland, where the *Fisher & Paykel* compound was located. I was impressed. The boat was very fast, and we had no equipment problems. I was offered the navigator's position on the boat.

Then the training started. We were at the gym at 6 AM, where our coach, Tony Ebert, put us through the paces, lifting weights, doing push-ups, and running. We then had a crew breakfast and meeting, hopped on the boat, and sailed all day, working on the boat's polars, sail crossovers, and crew work. This lasted until dark. We had dinner, went to bed, and started all over again the next day. We followed this schedule six days a week from February to June.

In June we took the boat apart and put it on a ship bound for Philadelphia. The crew all flew from Auckland to Philadelphia, where we put the boat back together. Coach Tony was there, and kept up our conditioning. One morning we ran through downtown Philadelphia to the museum where they filmed the movie *Rocky*, and we did pushups on the steps.

We sailed *F&P* down the Delaware River, out into the Atlantic Ocean, and up to Newport, Rhode Island. We stayed in Newport for a couple weeks, preparing the boat for the Transatlantic Race from Newport to Cork, Ireland.

The Transatlantic Race was wet and wild. On day four, a front came through, and we had thirty-five knots of wind on the nose. The seas built up, and we started flying off the waves and landed with bone-jarring crashes. We had to remove sail, until we had only a deep-reefed main up, and were doing just seven to eight knots of boat speed. After the front went through, we finally saw what the boat could do. Broad reaching in thirty-five to forty knots of wind with the small "chicken chute" up, the boat regularly surfed in the twenties, hitting thirty knots at times. The twenty-four-hour runs for those days were 314, 345, and 305 miles respectively.

Skipper Grant Dalton at the helm of F&P

As we neared Ireland, the wind died, and the sun came out. We sailed up the southeast coast to Cork in a light breeze, and crossed the finish line in eleven days and three hours. We were 400 miles ahead of the next boat, *NCB Ireland*, and we had broken *Kialoa III*'s transatlantic record by three hours.

We sailed the boat to Plymouth, England, where we set up a training camp at Queen's Battery Marina. The crew was put up in several houses in Noss Mayo, a quiet village on the Yealm River. The locals didn't know what to make of the invasion of their quiet village by the red-shirted, loud Kiwis. But we quickly found the local pub, and made friends with the townspeople.

Our physical training stepped up to a new level. We started working out with the Royal Marine Commandos at Stonehouse Barracks in Plymouth. We ran, jumped, climbed ropes, and did their obstacle course.

We even had marine drill instructors yelling at us. I felt like I had stood in the wrong line, and signed up for a Green Beret unit instead of a Whitbread boat.

Training with the Royal Marine Commandos in Plymouth

We sailed the boat to Ostende, Belgium, to race two Whitbread boats, *Equity and Law* from Holland, and *Rucanor Sport* from Belgium in the North Sea. It was a lot of fun. We stayed in Brugge, an ancient and very beautiful city. Besides racing, we did a lot of sightseeing, sat in the outdoor cafes, and drank some great beer. We also won the races, which was an added bonus.

Our final practice was the Fastnet Race, from Cowes, England around Fastnet Rock off Ireland, then back to the finish in Plymouth, and our first real confrontation with most of the Whitbread maxis. It was a light 400-mile beat into the wind from Cowes to the rock, and we expected the maxi sloops to get away from us. But much to our surprise, we were the first boat around Fastnet, with *Steinlager*, the other New Zealand ketch, second.

In what was a preview of the next nine months, *Steinlager* and *F&P* sailed side by side for hour after hour. In the end, *Steinlager* was first, beating us in by just three minutes.

Leg One – Portsmouth to Punta Del Este

The start was spectacular, with thousands of spectator boats filling the waters off Portsmouth, England. Twenty-four boats from fourteen countries started, including fourteen maxis around eighty feet in length. Conditions were ideal; sunny skies and a close reach in sixteen knots of wind, which came aft as the fleet passed Cowes. Spinnakers went up for the reach down the Solent and past the Needles.

With all the excitement of the start, we hadn't had much time to think about anything else. But as we settled down for the run across the English Channel to Ile d'Ouessant in north France, everyone on board was a bit quiet as they pondered the enormous undertaking ahead. Over the next nine months, we would race around the world, covering 33,000 miles through various trade winds, the steaming flat calms of the Doldrums, and the snow, icebergs and howling winds of the Southern Ocean.

The course had changed for the 1989/90 Whitbread Race. Instead of four legs, we would have six: Portsmouth, England; Punta del Este, Uruguay; Fremantle, Australia; Auckland, New Zealand; Punta del Este, Uruguay; Ft. Lauderdale, Florida, and finish at Portsmouth, England.

The passage out the English Channel and across the Bay of Biscay was a light run in 8-10 knots of wind; easy sailing, but with a lot of jibes. Then as we approached Cape Finesterre, the wind poured out of the Pyrenees and whipped around the corner of Spain in a venturi, increasing the wind to fifty knots. We set a storm spinnaker and small mizzen gennaker, and took off on a wild ride down the coast of Portugal.

Overleaf: F&P on a fast reach

Steinlager and *Merit* kept going west after Finesterre, while the bulk of the fleet, including us, sailed down the rhumb line off Portugal. The wind held for a couple days, then died down. *Steinlager* now 300 miles west, still had thirty-five knots of wind and steadily pulled ahead of the fleet.

The Azores High was situated very far north, so the trade winds expected off Madeira and the Canary Islands were virtually nonexistent. It was hot and sunny with a ten-knot breeze blowing from the northeast. It was great cruising weather, but we were racing and wanted wind, lots of wind! As we approached the Cape Verde Islands off Africa, the trades did finally fill in, and we enjoyed some good surfing.

As we headed southwest toward Brazil, it got hotter and hotter, and the wind started dying. At about ten degrees north, the trade winds fell apart, and we entered the Doldrums. There were periods of no wind interspersed with rain squalls producing twenty-five knots of wind. The temperature rose until it was like a sauna below deck, and sleeping became difficult. The crew started sleeping on the cabin sole near the companionway where they could find a bit of wind blown down by the sails.

The Doldrums let us off pretty easy. We sailed through them in two days with the knot meter reading all zeroes only a couple of times. The wind filled back in, and off Rio de Janeiro, it came aft and built to thirty-five knots. We took off surfing down the big seas, doing a steady twenty knots under the 1.5 ounce spinnaker.

About 1:00 AM, as I was lying in my bunk, I heard a loud crash. The boat shook violently, followed by the dreadful hail, "All hands on deck!" I ran up, looked after, and saw a twenty-foot stump where the mizzen mast used to be. Trailing behind the boat was fifty feet of mast, sails, and rigging.

I had a very strong sense of déjà vu. In the last Whitbread Race on *NZI Enterprise*, I had run on deck to see the same thing, but that time it was our main mast (and only mast) that had crumpled.

We dropped the spinnaker, put a line around the broken mizzen mast, and slowly winched it aboard. We disassembled it, and put the rigging and sails below. With the broken section secured on deck, we set the 2.5 ounce storm chute and took off surfing once again. The whole operation took under two hours. It was a pretty amazing recovery.

Once again we were racing, but now with about twenty percent less sail area. We were now *Fisher & Paykel* the sloop. As we sailed down the coast of Uruguay, we pushed the boat hard, so the other maxis wouldn't pass us. We crossed the finish line in Punta Del Este in third place behind *Steinlager* and the Swiss boat, *Merit*. The 6,000 mile leg took us twenty-seven days, with an average boat speed of nine knots.

Punta Del Este

Leg One was over. We were tired, but happy to be ashore, and we celebrated. Some of the crew celebrated a bit too much, and got into trouble with the authorities after getting very drunk and riding a "borrowed" bicycle into the harbor.

We spent the first week in Punta cleaning, putting in a new mizzen mast, and repairing the boat. The second week we got to go on vacation, to just get away from the boat and each other for a while.

Then we came back together as a crew, loaded on provisions, tuned the rigging, looked at new sails, and got used to the boat again. This was pretty much the schedule for each of the stopovers during the race.

Tragedy struck the fleet when the skipper of the Russian boat, *Fazisi*, went missing. Everyone thought he had defected. We had hosted a barbeque at our crew house, and invited the *Fazisi* crew.

There was a lot of Kiwi Lager, and the Russians brought vodka, and we shared toasts to each other. It was fun for us, and we could tell the Russians were having the time of their lives, experiencing a newfound freedom.

Fergie, the Duchess of York visits the yachts in Punta

The next day, their skipper, Alexej Gryshenko, who had gone missing, was found hanging by the neck in a tree not far from the yacht club. He had apparently committed suicide. It didn't make a lot of sense. He was married and had a three-month old daughter. Fazisi had done well, finishing sixth on the leg from England.

Skip Novak, the American working with *Fazisi*, said "Alexej took the race extremely serious, more serious than we ever imagined. He was very tired, and under extreme pressure from his superiors in the Soviet Union." We'll never know why he did it, but it was one of the great tragedies of the race.

I took off and visited Montevideo and Buenos Aires, and when I returned, there was another tragedy. Janne Gustaffson, the bowman on the Swedish boat, *The Card*, and one of the most well liked crew in the fleet, was in a motorcycle accident in Punta del Este and was killed. There was a cloak of sadness over the fleet, after losing two of our mates.

Just before the start of the next leg, there was a trophy presentation, and Fergie, the Duchess of York, flew in from England to hand out the trophies. We all go the meet, and talk with her. It was a bright spot in a rough period.

Leg Two – Punta Del Este to Fremantle

We left Punta del Este in light winds and dove south to get into the westerly winds pouring out of Cape Horn. The tactic paid off, and by day five we had taken the lead, and were firmly in the "Roaring Forties." It started to get cold quickly.

The wind was strong and filled with freezing rain and sleet. The temperature on deck was zero degrees Celsius, and we were wearing four layers of clothes, a balaclava on our heads, and waterproof mittens.

It was Cedric's birthday, and he received a gift of a bloody nose when the clew of a sail banged him in the face. There was a lot of blood, but it wasn't serious. Radar, the cook, made him a birthday treat of custard with his name written on it in chocolate.

The wind was blowing forty-five knots, and we had the small storm chute up, when the halyard block at the base of the mast broke. Without a proper lead to the winch, the halyard winch was levered off the deck, and went flying to the mast. It was a self-tailing winch, and actually went to the mast exit, and stopped.

Meanwhile, the spinnaker was twenty feet out from the masthead, and flogging like crazy. I thought we would lose the mast. But Matthew Smith, thinking quickly, pulled out his rigging knife, and cut the halyard free. The winch fell from the mast and bounced on the deck, and Matthew caught it before it went overboard. The spinnaker dropped into the water, and we ran over it. We pulled the chute aboard, set another spinnaker, and took off at twenty knots again. This was an example of how good the F&P crew were.

On day eight it started snowing, and we sighted our first iceberg. We radioed the other boats, and told them to keep a look out. Movement on the icy decks was extremely dangerous, and five crewmen on various boats went overboard during the leg. All were recovered, but Tony Phillips, off *Creighton's Naturally*, was dead after being in the water for twenty-five minutes.

It was another tragic loss to the fleet, and a powerful reminder just how close we are to danger and death. The incident brought home the importance of clipping on our life harnesses all the time.

On *Fisher & Paykel*, we were pushing the boat and sailing fast. We sailed an astounding 2,051 miles in six days, with twenty-four-hour runs, of 356, 337, 370, 362, 340, and 286 miles, made good to the finish.

We were in the lead as we approached Fremantle, Australia, and the finish. With only 300 miles to go, and the other boats catching up, Grant decided we had to lighten the boat. So we threw out all our food, except for some oatmeal. It looked like we would arrive the next day, and the oatmeal would give us energy for one day. Of course you know what happened, the wind died, and it took us two days to get in, and all we had to eat for breakfast, lunch, and dinner was oatmeal.

My journal read, "After 7,000 miles of sailing through 50+ knot storms, and 40-foot seas, and snow and icebergs, we're drifting on a hot, oily-calm sea." *Steinlager*, *Rothman's*, and *Merit*, saw our predicament, and sailed around us to the East. They beat us into Fremantle, and we ended up fourth.

It was a memorable leg, with extreme conditions, intensive racing, and the tragedy of the death of another of our fellow crewmen.

Fremantle, Australia

Fremantle was hot and sunny. What a nice change after the freezing Southern Ocean. We started to thaw out, and our depression over ending up fourth after leading most of the way slowly disappeared. After a few beers, it didn't seem to matter much. In fact one of our crew got so drunk, he wandered into the wrong house, thinking it was the *F&P* crew house. The Fremantle Yacht Club got a phone call from an elderly lady living across the street.

She said there was a young man in a *Fisher & Paykel* T-shirt asleep on her bed in her bedroom, and she asked if they wanted him back, or could she keep him.

In Fremantle, I met Jack Dures, one of the very experienced local sailors. He was quite interested in the Whitbread Race, and we became good friends. Jack was in his eighties, and had been sailing off Fremantle his whole life. I would see him swimming in the ocean in the early morning, and we would often have a beer together in the evening at the Cottesloe Hotel Pub. He invited me to the Royal Freshwater Yacht Club on the Swan River, and they made me an honorary member. Jack was wonderful. I learned of Western Australia through the eyes and memories, of an "old timer."

We got our week of vacation, and I rented a car, and drove south to the Margaret River region, which consisted of rolling green hills with beautiful beaches and valleys. It is similar in climate to Napa Valley in California and the residents there produce some great wines as well. I had fun visiting wineries and relaxing on the beach. I also visited a couple wildlife parks that were full of kangaroos, wallabies, emus, and wombats.

Leg Three – Fremantle to Auckland

Merit, F&P, and Steinlager starting Leg Three

It was raining and windy at the start off Fremantle. But it cleared up by the time we sailed down the west coast and reached Cape Leeuwin.

We had strong reaching conditions, which suited the big ketches, and we sailed very fast with *Steinlager* right next to us for hour after hour. We stayed together for day after day. I would come on deck after my off watch, and there she was. It was pretty exciting stuff, only boat lengths apart sailing in thirty to thirty-five knots of wind, catching waves and surfing to twenty-five knots of boat speed.

We celebrated Christmas south of Melbourne. Four years earlier I had celebrated Christmas on *NZI Enterprise* south of Tasmania, so it was almost a repeat. Radar cooked us a gourmet Christmas dinner of real turkey and stuffing. Our first non-freeze-dried meal on the boat ever!

As the boats approached Tasmania, *Charles Jourdan* was hit by a whale, or they may have hit the whale. It tore a hole in the side of the boat about two feet by six feet, and the fleet awaited anxiously to see if they needed help if the boat sank. Fortunately, the hole was above the water line, and they could repair it with good old duct tape, screws, and aluminum plate. They continued racing, but at a slower pace. When they arrived in Auckland, they were welcomed with a gift of an inflatable whale.

Crossing the Tasman Sea, *Union Bank of Finland* broke her mast. They managed to salvage the broken pieces and make a jury-rig. They cut down their sails, and continued racing. She looked like a native fishing boat when she crossed the finish line, but the crew deserved a lot of credit, they did what they needed to do to finish.

It was neck and neck between *F&P* and *Steinlager* as we approached Auckland. Fifteen miles north of Auckland, with Steinlager about 3 boat lengths ahead, a black line squall came in from the west. *Steinlager* started shortening sail, and we knew we should too, but we were catching her. This was our chance. Then the squall hit, and all hell broke loose. The wind went from twenty knots to forty-five knots, and came forward ninety degrees. We'd waited too long, and the boat was knocked flat in the water. By the time we got the sails down and new ones up, *Steinlager* had pulled out to a half mile lead that she held to the finish and beat us in by six minutes.

The welcome in Auckland was mind boggling. As we entered Auckland Harbor, we had to thread our way through a solid mass of spectator boats filled with well-wishers. Tamaki Drive was lined with cars honking their horns, and the wharves were covered with people. When we arrived at Prince's Wharf and tied up, there were 25,000 cheering Kiwis on the dock, bands playing, flags waving, and even fireworks.

Auckland, New Zealand

We were sports champions in New Zealand. There were nine hours of live television covering the finish. An estimated 250,000 people greeted us when we arrived. The Mayoress of Auckland put on a ticker tape parade down the main street for the crews of all the Whitbread boats. There were race programs with all the crew's pictures, and I signed hundreds of autographs. It was strange to me, a crewman from the United States, where sailing gets little press.

Lin and Coleen Carmichael put me up again in their lovely home in Brown's Bay. The Whitbread crews were celebrities in Auckland, and it was nice to find a quiet refuge at the Carmichael's.

For my week vacation, I visited the North Island, staying in Whakatane, then Rotorua, and Turangi. Another example of the incredible Kiwi hospitality happened here. I had met Paul Green, chief ranger at the Tongariro National Park, at the Carmichael's in Auckland. He said, "We are going to be in Auckland while you are visiting Turangi, why don't you use our house?" So, I did, and when I drove into their driveway and opened their house to put my bags in, a little old lady came running up and said, "Who are you, and what are you doing going in to the Green's house?" I told her, and she went away. A few minutes later there was a knock on the door, and it was the same lady. She said her name was Belle, and she lived next door. She apologized for being so unneighborly, and she wanted to welcome me, so she made me a pot of tea and biscuits.

The next morning at 5:30 AM there was a knock on the door, and there was a man decked out in fishing gear, complete with trout flies in his hat. He said his name was Brian Campbell, and Paul Green had called and said I might like to go fishing.

Auckland put on a ticker tape parade for the crews.

So, off we went. We met his brother, Don Campbell, a fishing guide, and took off in his boat on Lake Taupo. We went sightseeing for a couple hours, caught a few trout, and then pulled up on a beach for a cup of tea. They had forgotten cups, so Brian went to ask a Maori lady watching some children playing in the lake, if she might have a couple cups we could borrow. They went up to her beach shack, and shortly called Don and I up. Pretty soon the whole family was there and we were having lunch with them. It seems Kiwi hospitality is universal in New Zealand.

Leg Four – Auckland to Punta Del Este

The start was a madhouse with over 400,000 New Zealanders lining the shores, hills, and islands of the Hauraki Gulf. over 15,000 boats filled the water as well. The gulf became a washing machine with the wakes of all the spectator boats; and our biggest concern was to get out of Auckland without hitting a well-meaning spectator.

And the inevitable happened; just ten minutes after the start, the Swedish boat, *The Card*, sailed into the spectator fleet, caught her mizzen mast with that of an anchored boat, and ripped *The Card's* mast out of the boat. They cut the broken mast away, threw it overboard, and continued racing as a sloop.

Once we rounded the Coromandel Peninsula, the wind filled in and we headed south, looking for the big winds in the "Roaring Forties." But instead of the strong winds we had in Leg Two, we only found fifteen to twenty knots. We carried a spinnaker, staysail, full main, mizzen gennaker and full mizzen for days on end.

We hadn't planned to sail south of 58 degrees, but when we reached 58 degrees, the weather forced us south. To sail fast, we had to sail south or jibe north on a bad course. So south we went, past 60 degrees, then 61, and then 62 degrees.

Now we had another problem, ice. It became very cold, and we started seeing icebergs. At first, we saw just one on the horizon, then two or three at a time, until we had six bergs in sight at one time. We put a crewman on the bow watching for bergs and growlers, the small pieces that barely show about the water.

Then after eighteen days, out of the mist appeared Cape Horn. It was a dreary and rainy morning, an appropriate backdrop for this infamous piece of land that had claimed the lives of so many sailors over the centuries.

As we rounded the Horn, we could feel the presence of lost sailors and ships. It was eerie. But it was also a celebration. Rounding Cape Horn is a milestone in a sailor's life. It's kind of a rite of passage from being a sailor to being a "salt."

Sailing fast in the Southern Ocean

We sailed through the Straits of Le Maire and passed the Falkland Islands. The wind stayed light and on the nose for the 1,000 mile trip to Punta del Este.

As we sailed north, the temperature started rising, and Andy decided to change his socks for the first time in twenty days. I thought we might all die from the stench, but luckily someone grabbed the socks and threw them overboard.

As we were approaching the finish with *Steinlager*, there was a tragedy happening just north of the Falkland Islands. The 81-foot Finnish boat, *Martela*, lost its keel and turned over. Luckily *Merit* and *Charles Jourdan* we close by, and managed to pick up all the crew. No one was lost or hurt.

We crossed the finish line in Punta just twenty-one minutes behind *Steinlager*.

Rounding Cape Horn

Punta Del Este Again

Being one of the few Americans in the race, I was asked to make a trip to Washington, DC, and New York to promote the Whitbread Race coming to the United States for the first time. So, Joe English, the skipper of *NCB Ireland*, and I flew to New York, and met Talbot Wilson, who was heading the promotional tour.

It was a wild, mad dash through New York and Washington with a dozen interviews and meetings in just two days. We had interviews with reporters from *Newsday* and the *Boston Globe*.

We went to the United Nations, and met the Secretary General, Javier Perez de Cuellar and gave him a Whitbread flag. He gave us a United Nations flag. We had lunch with reporters from AP, UPI, Reuters, EFE (Spain), and DPE (Germany). Then we appeared on the CBS show called *International Dateline*.

Joe English, U.N. Secretary General, and John Jourdane

The next day was spent in Washington, DC, where we went to the National Press Club for interviews with *USA Today*, *Washington Post*, *Baltimore Sun*, *West Palm Beach Post*, New Zealand Wire Service, and the international TV group VISNET.

It was Joe's first trip to Washington, so we gave him a quick tour of the Washington monuments. Then it was off to New York and a connecting twelve-hour flight to Punta del Este. The whole thing happened so fast, it seemed like a dream.

Leg Five – Punta del Este to Fort Lauderdale

The weather was beautiful at the start. The wind was blowing ten knots out of the north, so it was a beat up the coast of Uruguay and Brazil. The temperature rose dramatically as we entered the tropics. It became very hot below deck, and it was difficult to sleep.

Once we rounded the eastern corner of Brazil, the wind came aft, we put up all our big sails, and took off. It was a beautiful sail across the top of Brazil, reaching fifteen to twenty knots of wind on course for the Bahamas. Brazil is huge. We sailed along its coastline for thirteen days of the twenty-two day leg of the race.

For the next several days we sailed along the Caribbean in beautiful trade winds. The two Kiwi ketches literally sailed away from the fleet, and by the time we reached the Bahamas we were neck and neck 100 miles ahead of the next boat. This was what yachting was supposed to be like, not snow on the deck or steamy Doldrums. The crew morale was high.

A front came through as we entered the Providence Channel and headed for the finish. The wind built and came aft. With our large spinnaker and mizzen gennaker up in twenty-five to thirty knots of wind, we flew across the Gulf Stream, averaging sixteen knots of boat speed for the last fifty miles.

Steinlager crossed the finish line off Fort Lauderdale at 3:40 AM on a very rainy morning. We finished thirty-four minutes later.

Fort Lauderdale put on a great reception for all the boats, and we were made to feel at home. As I was being interviewed by reporters on our arrival, I was asked, "How does it feel to be the first American to ever finish a Whitbread Race on U.S. soil?" I hadn't thought about it before that moment and said "I am very honored."

Fort Lauderdale, Florida

The crews of all the boats really enjoyed Fort Lauderdale. The city went out of its way to make our stay enjoyable. Most the hotels and bars put on parties and offered free drinks for the crews, and one even offered free sports massage for any Whitbread crewman. It was also Spring Break, and the town was loaded with pretty suntanned, bikini-clad coeds. For the Whitbread crewmen who had been at sea for eight months with a bunch of men, it was like they had died and gone to heaven.

One evening, I was having a beer at the Bahia Cabana bar with a few friends. I looked around the table and realized that this is what the Whitbread is really all about. Sitting at the table with me was Yuki from Russia, Magnus from Sweden, Tracy from England, Patrick from Ireland, Steve from New Zealand, and Cedric from Australia. This was truly an international gathering, where men and women from all over the world came together as friends.

There was a lot of press and television coverage of the Race in Florida, and being one of the few Americans in the Race, it was becoming hard to find peace and quiet. So, when my week of vacation arrived, I got out of town. I went to Turtle Cay in the Bahamas with my friend Annie Ritterbusch. It was perfect, no telephones, no TV, and no newspapers. We just swam, snorkeled, sailed a little dinghy, read, walked on the beach, and watched the sunsets.

Leg Six – Ft. Lauderdale to Portsmouth, England

After a great send off by a couple thousand spectator boats in Fort Lauderdale, we had a great run up the East Coast in the Gulf Stream. With a three-knot current and the wind from aft, we averaged fourteen knots over the bottom. It was shorts and T-shirt sailing.

Silver Bullet, John DeLaura's Santa Cruz 70 from Long Beach, sailed the leg unofficially, and was quite impressive in the first few days, as we sailed in Transpac-like conditions. *Bullet* was very fast, and was right up with the leaders, but then the wind lightened and came forward, and the maxis took off.

The boats and crews were tired. They had been racing for nine months and almost 30,000 miles. *Gatorade,* the Italian entry (the former *NZI Enterprise*), broke a spreader the first night out, and put into St. Augustine, Florida, to fix it. The second night, *Rothmans* snapped an upper intermediate shroud, and almost lost its mast. They sailed into Charleston, South Carolina, to fix it.

Two days later it was *Steinlager's* turn when the port mizzen chain plate pulled out of the hull. Helmsman Brad Butterworth, thinking very quickly, turned the wheel, jibed the boat, and the saved the mainmast and mizzen from going overboard. The crew cut up one of the engine mounts, used it as a backing plate, and re-bolted the chain plate to the hull.

Six days out of Florida, *Satquote British Defender* broke its mast when a shroud pulled out of a spreader. They jury-rigged the stump and continued racing.

A couple of very tired pigeons landed on deck one day. They had leg bands that said they were from Miami. Ceddy adopted the birds, and named them Gentle Annie and Mr. Fussy, after the brand names of Fisher & Paykel's washing machine and dish washer. He built them a little bird house behind the helmsman's cockpit and fed them porridge and crackers. They gained strength and health, then one day flew off toward land. I hope they had a good sense of direction, because they landed on the boat when we were off Georgia, and when they left we were off Nova Scotia.

About half way across the Atlantic we sailed out of the Gulf Stream and into the Labrador Current. The water temperature dropped from 67 degrees to 37 degrees in thirty minutes. The air temperature plummeted also, and a sea fog developed. The cold water was a signal that we were entering iceberg country, and we soon saw one. Our quick, easy sail to England was deteriorating rapidly.

Ceddy and Gentle Annie

A low pressure system formed north of the Azores, and gave us head-winds and cold, rainy weather. It was a slow-moving depression, and stayed just ahead of us, giving us rain and headwinds for the next seven days. It was a long, hard slog, and it made the leg seem quite long.

As we approached Lizard Point on the southwest corner of England, *Steinlager* and *F & P* were sailing dead even again, in light air. It was amazing how even in speed we were. We traded the lead over and over, and then once again *Steinlager* pulled ahead, sailed into the Solent, and finished ahead of us.

The Royal Army howitzers boomed as we crossed the finish line in Southampton. We jumped up and down, shook each others hands, shouted with joy, and drank champagne. We had raced right around the world, pushing the boat and ourselves to the limit in all conditions. I was tired, exhausted, drained, but incredibly satisfied, and felt a real sense of achievement and fulfillment.

Fifteen

Blondie's Pacific Power Trip

Blondie—Santa Cruz 70
Owner—Peter Tong
Crew—Dave Ullman, John Jourdane, Pete Frazier, Craig Chamberlain,
Sarah Tong, Ross Field, Randy Smith, Phil Ramming,
Tom Burch, Drew Martin, Allan Vaught

When I was doing the Whitbread Race on *Fisher & Paykel*, Pat Farrah sold *Blondie* to Peter Tong. And when I returned to California, Peter asked me to run *Blondie* for him. Peter was another great owner. We had a lot of fun racing the boat up and down the West Coast, and then to Hawaii in the 1991 Transpac Race.

The Transpac crew included Dave Ullman, Randy Smith, Craig Chamberlain, Sarah Tong, Tom Burch, Tim, and Pete Frazier, Ross Field, Phil Ramming, Drew Martin and Alla Vaught. We had a great sail, and wonderful time in Honolulu.

My delivery crew flew in, and we prepared the boat for the return crossing to Long Beach. But what was supposed to be a routine Transpac return delivery, turned out to being anything but normal.

We were 100 miles out of Oahu, on the way back, sailing in twenty-five knots of wind with a reefed delivery main and a small working jib, when I heard a loud bang.

Opposite: Blondie sailing into the Ala Wai Yacht Harbor in Honolulu.

I looked forward, and saw the mast slowly collapsing to leeward. I called all hands, which wasn't necessary, because they were already on the way up. I ran forward through a tangle of rigging, sails, and lines.

There was an ugly pounding and scraping sound coming from under the bow, where the mast was hitting the hull, so I decided to jettison the rig before it punched a hole in the boat. We pulled the pins at the chain plates, cut away the halyards and sheets, and then slashed away at the mainsail.

Cutting away the mainsail

The whole rig was free except for the port vertical shrouds, which were held by the one remaining spreader. We decided to cut the V-2 shroud, a great idea in theory, but on *Blondie* the V-2 was cobalt-stainless steel, which is extremely hard. First, we tried cutting it with the big Felco wire cutters with Dave, Mark, and I all pushing them closed. We only ended up bending the cutter handles, and didn't do anything to the cobalt rod. Then we got out the hacksaw with carbide blades, but after twenty minutes of non-stop sawing, with the three of us taking turns, we had only scratched the surface. Finally, we got a big hammer and a drift pin, and pounded out the clevis pin holding the shroud. The whole rig fell away from the boat and headed for the ocean bottom, some 3 miles below.

Powering back to Honolulu

We pulled in all the trailing sheets and lines, fired up the engine and started motoring back to Honolulu. I had about twelve hours to think about what we should do next. By the time we tied up at the Ala Wai Yacht Harbor, I had pretty much determined that we had three options: wait for a new mast to arrive and sail the boat home; put the boat on a barge and ship it home; or jury-rig the stump of the mast we had left, put on a steadying sail and a lot of diesel, and power the boat home.

After several long telephone conversations with the insurance company, and Blondie's owner Peter Tong, we chose the latter: motor the boat back to Long Beach. It was actually a pretty easy decision since it would take two or three months to build a new mast and ship it to Hawaii, then we would have to sail the boat back with an untested rig. And after hearing about all the damage the yacht Taxi Dancer sustained being barged back from Hawaii after the previous Transpac, I decided that pulling Blondie out, putting her on a makeshift cradle, and shipping her home on a rolling barge; out of my control; was way too scary. That left only the third option, to power the boat home 2,500 miles across the Pacific.

I told the delivery crew my decision. Ron Dillehey and Mary Smith felt they couldn't afford the time off work to do the second delivery. Mark Donohue was all for it; Dave Scudder couldn't go, but would help us get ready. So we started preparing Blondie for her big motorboat ride; and the Honolulu sailing community turned out in force to lend a hand. Ala Wai Marine (also known as "Pirate Pete's"), pulled our stump of a mast out of the boat, and helped us build a new masthead plate to hold a head stay, back stays and halyards. Bruce Vasconcellos rounded up 500 gallons of plastic containers to hold all the fuel we would need. Fuzz Foster of North Sails cut down our storm trysail to fit our new low aspect sail plan as a steadying sail. We installed a VHF antenna and an all-around light on the new masthead, and an SSB antenna on one of the back stays.

I serviced the engine, shopped around for a complete set of engine spares, a lot of engine oil, coolant, and battery water. We loaded on 600 gallons of diesel fuel in thirty and fifty-five gallon plastic barrels in the cockpit and down below around the mast. We filled the water tanks with 200 gallons of water, and loaded on thirty days worth of provisions, fishing lines, and lots of CDs and books.

We found our third crewman in Ward Neale, who was working on the Japanese yacht, *Marishiten*, a Nelson Marek 68, sailing back to Japan. Ward had some free time before that boat was leaving for Japan, and decided to go with us. So with an international crew of three; Mark from Canada, Ward from New Zealand, and myself from the United States, we headed off across the Pacific on the U.L.D.P (ultra light displacement powerboat), *Blondie*.

Blondie the Powerboat

The following are a few excerpts from my log during the crossing:

Wednesday, July 24, Day One: It was a bumpy ride last night. The seas aren't big, only 4—5 feet, but they are short and confused. The boat has a completely different motion than while sailing. It rolls with the swell, then the keel takes over, and it jerks back. It'll take a while to get used to that. The engine is running smoothly; we're doing 7 knots at 1,900 rpm. The watch system is really easy; I'm on the helm for three hours; then Ward is on for three hours; followed by Mark. So it's three on and six off. We are getting a lot of rest and reading a lot of books.

Friday, July 26, Day Three: The wind has picked up to 25 knots with confused seas. The boat is pounding a lot as we try to steer around the short, steep waves. It's been one of those days; I shouldn't have gotten out of my bunk. The refrigerator has stopped working, unfortunately with two weeks of frozen food in it. Then the stereo died. The crew says they can get by without food, but they have to have music. We worked on both units all-day finally getting the stereo running, but the reefer is down for the duration. We caught a nice 15-pound mahimahi, so we won't starve for at least another day.

Sunday, July 28, Day Five: We shut down the engine every day to check the fluids and transfer fuel with a 12-volt pump. I haven't quite figured out how to prime the pump right, and usually manage to get diesel all over myself, the boat, and anyone standing nearby. Then I have to clean the decks and jump in the water to take a bath. We have a dilemma; what do we do with all the food that's rapidly decaying in the refrigerator? One faction onboard says lets eat it all now, and we won't have to eat for the next couple weeks. I'm leaning toward the other faction, which says to put it in a sealed trash bag, and set it adrift with a note that says, "For the poor people in China."

The big albacore

Tuesday, July 30, Day Seven: We passed the halfway point today. I shut down the engine and did a complete service on it; changing the oil, filters, etc. In the middle of the "Jiffy Lube," there was a loud commotion on deck with Mark yelling and cursing. I ran up to see him wrestling with a huge albacore. It seemed as big as he was. He had it on the deck in a hammerlock, and was trying to kill it by pouring Cutty Sark Scotch down its gills. This method usually kills the fish without bloodshed, but this fish was tough. It got Mark in a reverse body slam and almost had him pinned. I got to them just as the fish was trying to pour whiskey down Mark's ear. With a winch handle, I finished him off (the fish, not Mark), and we gorged ourselves on fresh tuna for the next two days.

Friday, August 2, Day 10: The boat is getting lighter as we use up the diesel. It feels livelier, and there is a noticeable increase in speed. It's amazing how tuned in to the engine I've become, since it's our lifeline. I listen to every change in sound and vibration, constantly monitor the gauges, and do daily checks for fluid loss and chafe on the belts.

Monday, August 5, Day 13: It's been a whale of a morning. There are gray whales migrating south for the winter. I've sighted 15 of them, some as big as *Blondie*. I had a narrow miss with one when I tied the wheel off and was peeing off the transom. I turned around and saw huge whale bearing down on our beam, only 50 ft. away. I ran to the wheel and tried to turn, only to remember I had tied it off. As I fumbled with the knot, I awaited the inevitable crash with the leviathan. Somehow, I got the wheel untied, turned it hard to port, and missed the whale by inches. I think I scared the whale as much as it scared me. It sounded immediately, with the flukes just grazing our transom, as it slid beneath the waves.

Tuesday, August 6, Day 14: We were met at the Point Firman buoy in San Pedro by Peter Tong, *Blondie*'s owner on his Peter's powerboat, *Moxie*. They passed us fresh sandwiches, ice cold fruit, and Rum and Cokes. What a treat after 11 days with no refrigeration! It turned out to be an enjoyable trip, although a bit noisy. But next time, I think I will do it under sail.

Sixteen

The Route of Discovery Race
Pyewacket (Euro Disney) –
Huelva, Spain to the New World

Pyewacket—Santa Cruz 70
Owner—Roy E. Disney
Crew—Robbie Haines, Gary Weisman, Mark Rudiger, John Jourdane,
Roy P. Disney, Tim Disney, Scott Vogel, Gregg Hedrick, and Zan Drejes

In 1992, to commemorate the 500th anniversary of Christopher Columbus's voyage to New World, the Spanish government sponsored a race across the Atlantic Ocean. They invited boats from all over Europe and America to retrace old Chris's epic route, and billed it as the "greatest voyage since 1492." The 4,100-mile course would take the boats from Huelva in southern Spain (where Columbus started), to a waypoint in the Canary Islands (where Chris spent a few weeks and fell in love with the local governor's widow), to a waypoint in San Salvador Island in the Bahamas (which Chris thought was an island just off of Japan), to the finish line in Miami (which Chris never visited).

Roy Disney decided to do the race on his Santa Cruz 70, *Pyewacket*, and it took most of 1992 to sail *Pyewacket* to Spain. She sailed down the West Coast, through the Panama Canal, up the East Coast, and then across the pond to Ireland, where she did the Cork Race Week before heading to Jerez, Spain.

The *Pyewacket* crew arrived in Puerto Sherry to prepare the boat. It was an offshore racing "Dream Team" consisting of three Disneys (father Roy E. and sons Roy P. and Tim), two top sail makers/tacticians (Robbie Haines and Gary Weisman), two top navigators (Mark Rudiger and John Jourdane), a top yacht designer, Scott Vogel, and two top all-around offshore sailors (Gregg Hedrick and Zan Drejes). In a slow moment, someone figured out this group had collectively raced in fifty-seven Transpac Races!

The Pyewacket "Dream Team"

Our competition for the race was awesome. It included three maxis that had just completed the Whitbread Race: *Merit* (81-foot Farr maxi), *Publiespana* (the former *Fisher & Paykel*, 82-foot Farr maxi ketch), *Fortuna*

(82-foot maxi ketch), and *Brooksfield* (a brand new Italian Whitbread 60). Sitting in Puerto Sherry next to these Whitbread battlewagons, our Santa Cruz 70 seemed downright tiny. Besides the six level-rated maxis, an assortment of ten IMS and IOR boats, including an old Farr one tonner, were entered.

The start of the race was quite a mess. The afternoon before the start, when we should have been loading on last minute provisions, we had to do a twelve-mile "Media Race" around Cadiz Harbor in no wind. Then on the morning of the start, we had to motor five hours from Puerto Sherry to Huelva, then several miles up a river to Palos de la Frontera for a boat parade in front of the Columbus Monument. The boats passed in front of Christopher's statue while a band played each boat's national anthem. Next, we motored several miles back down the river to the starting area off the Huelva Jetty. Eventually, some nine hours after leaving the dock, we got a starting gun, but it wasn't that easy. After crossing the starting line, we had to sail an eight-mile triangle off Huelva, so the local population could watch the entries racing. Again there was no wind, and after sailing the triangle, we recrossed the starting line, in the opposite direction and finally headed on course for the Canary Islands. By the time we finally started, the crew was exhausted.

There was a large high pressure system sitting right over Spain, and the wind was almost nonexistent. The first several days were very light, and the sailing was frustrating. Someone figured our ETA at the present rate would put us in Miami about Easter. There was real concern about getting home in time for Christmas. And just as they did on the *Nina*, *Pinta*, and *Santa Maria*, our crew started talking mutiny; the possibility of hopping on a 747 in the Canary Islands came up more than once.

About five days into the race, the wind filled in, and came aft, and our big Mickey Mouse spinnaker went up. As soon as the boat started surfing, everyone forgot about stopping in the Canaries. We were sailing fast, and in second place behind *Merit*.

Pyewacket was renamed EuroDisney for the race

Then we faced another one of the race committee's idiosyncrasies. They wouldn't let us just sail by the island of Gran Canaria and check in. We had to sail down the east side of the island, into the port of Las Palmas, past the jetties, right to the sea wall, around an anchored navy boat, back out the harbor, and then beat back up the east side of the island to get back on course to the Bahamas. It was crazy!

The big ketches sailed north of the island of Tenerife to avoid the lee side and no wind to the south. We decided to sail between Gran Canaria and Tenerife, figuring that the direction of the wind would make a small lee. Our hunch paid off; the breeze was strong between the islands, and there was virtually no hole. We flew by Tenerife on a broad reach, and reclaimed the lead from *Merit*.

Three Disneys: Tim, Roy, and Roy Pat

For the next several days the wind was strong out of the East, and we experienced fast surfing conditions. It was great sailing in shorts and T-shirts, just like Transpac. We maintained our lead over *Merit*, and there were big smiles on everyone's faces.

Our fishermen, Gary and Gregg, put out a line and quickly reeled in a nice bonito and a huge albacore. We feasted on fresh fish for two days. What a pleasant change from freeze-dried food, frozen omelets and Power Bars!

As the boat historian, I began daily readings from Columbus's log. The crew actually enjoyed them, and occasionally threw out comments about how our two trips were alike (no wind, dried biscuits, and mutinous mumblings), and how they differed (sadly, we carried no casks of wine).

Zan in his racing P.J.'s

Zan appeared on deck in his spiffy sailing apparel, bright blue plaid flannel pajamas. He said they were passed down from his father, who supposedly always wore them on ocean crossings, and considered them lucky. They were actually quite stylish, and may become the rage in sailing gear. But as we sailed south, and the weather became warmer and warmer, the sleeves of the pajamas were chopped off, followed by the legs of the trousers. Finally, what remained of the "lucky" outfit was offered to the sea.

The fun downwind sailing didn't last long. This was the Atlantic Ocean, not the Pacific. The weather reports were showing a fierce winter storm pummeling the East Coast of the United States, and it was heading our way. When it arrived, the wind clocked to the south, then to the west, right on our nose. We steadily shortened sail and reefed as the wind and seas built until it was blowing a steady forty knots with gusts to forty-five.

Eurodisney sailing under storm trysail and storm jib

The boat kept going too fast, launching off the fifteen-foot waves and landing in the troughs with bone-jarring crashes. At one point, we actually put out lines as a drogue behind the boat and went bare-poles as the wind went over fifty knots. Then we put up the storm trysail and storm jib. It was a good combination, and kept the boat moving on course, but not moving so fast that it flew off the steep seas.

The front passed through, but just as we were breathing a sigh of relief, a second front approached. Again, the wind clocked around and built, but we were better prepared for it the second time, and shortened sail early. It wasn't so bad, but unfortunately, the powerful ketches, *Merit* and *Publiespana* reveled in these conditions, taking the lead back from us.

After the second front passed, the wind came out of the north to a reach. We cracked sheets, and soon we were blasting along at thirteen knots under a #3 jib and double-reefed main. We were pressing the boat hard on the morning of the eighteenth day when, all of the sudden, there was a loud snapping sound and the helm went very light. Gregg started to run below to see if the steering cable had snapped. Gary looked aft and said, "Forget it, Gregg." We watched helplessly as our ultra light carbon fiber rudder floated away. Both the rudder post and blade had inexplicably snapped off eighteen inches below the waterline.

We dropped the sails while Mark and Zan rigged up our emergency rudder, which was attached externally to a track on the transom. It's a great system theoretically, but we soon learned a lot about "rudder reality." The rudder blade was too short, and when we heeled, only about two feet of the blade stayed in the water. And the attachment to the boat was too short, only about a foot and a half of track concentrating all of the load to three spinnaker cars. The system lasted about an hour before breaking. The track bent and the spinnaker cars snapped. Lesson learned: the emergency rudder needs to be as strong as the original rudder, with a well-engineered attachment to the boat.

Luckily, we still had the eighteen inches of our original rudder. We found we could sail downwind with some control without a spinnaker and with the main and jib wung out, and the boat kept flat. This config-uration would not allow us to sail the last 500 miles through the Bahamas to the finish line, so we started looking for alternatives. The closest island with an airstrip where Roy's plane could fly in a replacement rudder was Grand Turk Island in the Turks and Caicos, just north of Haiti, and 150 miles dead downwind of our position.

The wind was still blowing strong, and we had a wild, edge-of-control ride to Grand Turk. Wing and wing with a #5 jib and two reefs in the main, but the boat was still hitting sixteen knots on the surfs. It took total concentration on the part of the helmsman to keep from broaching.

The Pyewacket crew leaving Turks & Caicos

We finally made landfall at Grand Turk Island, and anchored in the roadstead off Georgetown. A local diver named Harvey came out in his tiny twelve-foot boat and ferried the crew ashore, nine of us with all our gear, in one load. It was probably the scariest part of the whole voyage. Roy and Gregg went through the customs formalities, after which we had a real meal at the Oceanview Restaurant, where the crew savored "cheeseburgers in paradise," washed down with ice-cold Beck's Beer.

We toasted each other and our competitors (my old Whitbread boat, now called *Publiespana*, went on to win, with *Merit* second and *Fortuna* third). We also toasted old Christopher himself, after all, he made it to the New World, and we didn't. The next day we exercised an option Columbus never even dreamed about; we hopped on Disney's luxurious corporate jet and flew home.

Seventeen

Silver Bullet – Transpac 1993
First to Finish, First Overall

Silver Bullet—Santa Cruz 70
Owner—John DeLaura
Crew—Jeff Madrigali, Mark Rudiger, John Jourdane, Robert Flowerman,
Mike Howard, Curtis Blewett, Mark Sims, Dave Gruver.

The Transpac Race is the unofficial "granddaddy" of long-distance ocean races, and has been run every two years since its inception in 1906 to celebrate the birthday of Hawaii's King David Kalakaua. It was supposed to start in San Francisco in 1905, but the big earthquake messed up the plans, so they moved it to San Pedro, California, where it has been started most of the time since.

1993 was a year of changes for Transpac. In order to attract more entries, the race was opened up to PHRF (Performance Handicap Racing Fleet) entries for the first time. Boats as small as J/35s, and as large as the 102-foot Canadian training ship, *HMSC Oriole*, made the Pacific crossing to Oahu. *Rage*, a 70-foot Tom Wylie design from Portland, Oregon, didn't measure into any of the established classes, and opted to cut down on sail area so she could join the fleet. *Rage* ended up winning the PHRF fleet.

Opposite: Silver Bullet surfing to Honolulu

The Transpac Yacht Club also opted to stagger the start over four days for the first time; a move that allowed all the boats to arrive in Honolulu about the same time. The club also took a proactive stance for a cleaner ocean. All trash was kept aboard the vessels and picked up for recycling at the Ala Wai Yacht Harbor. For the first time, the slower boats didn't have the usual trail of trash to follow all the way to Hawaii.

The ongoing attraction of the Transpac is its abundance of spinnaker running in the strong trade winds, and of course the flower lei and mai tai greetings in palm-covered Waikiki. With a proclivity for high speed surfing, the race prompted the evolution of a whole new design of boat, the ultra light displacement boat (ULDB), or sled.

Transpac race tactics are determined by one weather feature, the North Pacific high. This high pressure system creates and controls the trade winds, and the winning boats are those that best anticipate its movement, intensity, and relationship to the Low pressure systems over Utah, Nevada, and Arizona.

The shortest course from Los Angeles to Honolulu is the great circle route, an arc with its center about 100 miles north of the rhumb line. This is the shortest course, but generally not the fastest because the North Pacific high is usually situated too close, and the winds in the center of the high are very light or non-existent. The winning strategy is to sail hard on the wind for the first two to three days to get across the ridge and into the trade wind belt as soon as possible. Then the navigator must locate the pressure isobar with the strongest wind (what Stan Honey calls "the best slot car slot"), and sail down that isobar south of the High. The wind generally clocks until the best jibe angle is reached for the sail into Honolulu. This strategy may sound easy, but the high is not stationary for long; it keeps moving, splitting, and changing, forcing the navigators to constantly adjust their courses.

Silver Bullet crossing the Diamond Head finish line.

The weather in 1993 was very atypical, with the high moving very far north, and remaining stationary. Most of the fleet chose a northern track with the shortest distance and strongest wind.

John DeLaura had put together a great crew for the 1993 race. Jeff Madrigali was the tactician, there were co navigators Mark Rudiger and John Jourdane. The crew was some of the best on the West Coast: Mike

Howard, Mark Sims, Curtis Blewett, Bill Erkelens, and Dave Gruver

After the start, Mark, Jeff, and I decided that north was the way to go, and it was worth the gamble to sail the shorter great circle route. If we could get out in front of the fleet by sailing less distance in more wind, then when the easterly shift came, we could jibe across in front of the fleet. It sounded good in theory, and we were going to stick to it.

The normal, steady trade winds were not present. Instead there were a lot of squalls and streaks of wind throughout the course.

On the third day we were the most northerly boat with Roy Disney's *Pyewacket* visible just to the south of us. A huge rain squall came through and we were lucky to be on the right side of it with a lot of wind. *Pyewacket* was unfortunate to be on the wrong side and was becalmed. At roll call the next morning, we were thirty miles ahead of *Pyewacket*.

The two fifty-footers, Neil Barth's *Persuasion* and Hasso Platner's *Morning Glory*, started twenty-four hours ahead of us, and they were the only two boats ahead of us as we approached Hawaii. The last night we passed *Morning Glory*, and early on the last morning we sailed up to *Persuasion*. As we passed them, while surfing at over twenty knots, we yelled over, "Excuse us, playing through." They didn't think it was funny.

With her red and white spinnaker tinted gold by the fading sunset, the big 70-footer ghosted past Diamond Head Lighthouse to the cheers of "Aloha" from an enthusiastic spectator fleet. *Silver Bullet* had just won the coveted Barn Door Trophy given to the elapsed time winner in the 2,225-mile Transpac Race from Los Angeles to Honolulu. The next boat to finish was *Persuasion*, an hour and a half later.

We motored into the coveted first slip on Transpac Row in the Ala Wai Yacht Harbor and were greeted by Hawaiian music, grass-skirted wives and girl friends, and lots of ice cold mai tais.

The Transpac Barn Door Trophy for First to Finish.

As a post script, we not only were first to finish and first in class and fleet, but we won the Ecology Trophy for saving all our trash, and ending up with only four full bags after eight days of racing with ten crew aboard.

Eighteen

Carpe Diem –
The Micronesian Milk Run

Carpe Diem—Tayana 42
Owners—Rex and Clarie Kosack
Crew—John Jourdane, Richie Saunders, Ben Bland, Steve Soenke,
Nick Kosack, and Vanessa Kosack.

Continental Airlines had a flight every other day from Honolulu to Johnston Island, Majuro, Kwajalein Atoll, Ponape, Truk, and Guam. They called it the *Milk Run* because they delivered milk and newspapers to the military bases on the islands. When the opportunity came up to deliver the Tyana 42, *Carpe Diem* from Honolulu to Saipan along the Milk Run, I jumped at the chance. Not only could I sail among the beautiful islands of Micronesia, but it should be a pleasant downwind voyage in the tropical trade winds.

In 1994, I was sailing in Mexico, and flew to Honolulu, and was met by the owners, Rex and Clarie Kosak. We went to the boat at Ala Wai Marine Harbor in Waikiki. It was a nice looking boat, really loaded with gear, but torn apart and under repair.

Opposite: Carpe Diem sailing to Majuro

The surveyor had found a cracked chain plate, so all the chain plates were being replaced. It was a major job. The boat was built around them, and they had to be dug out of the teak trim on the gunwales.

I read the Coast Pilot for the area we were sailing to, and learned a lot. Micronesia is a Greek word for small islands, and that is what they are. There are 1400 of them with a total land area of only 1060 square miles spread out over 4 million square miles of Pacific Ocean. Most of the islands are true atolls (islands surrounded by coral reef with a lagoon inside the reef). The climate is warm, but tempered by the trade winds. Rain is adequate but not over abundant.

We left the Ala Wai Yacht Harbor in Honolulu with a crew of four; the owners, Rex and Clarie Kosak, Richie Saunders, and me. A strong northeast trade wind was blowing twenty to twenty-five knots, with seas running about six to eight feet from the northeast also. Our course to Johnston Atoll was west southwest, so we were running dead down wind.

Our canoe-stern didn't like running dead down in large swells, and took on a violent roll. After a few hours of picking everyone up off the cabin sole several times, we decided we couldn't sail course, and we sheeted in and steered a broad reach. The motion was much better.

Our course would take us first 1,987 miles from Honolulu to Majuro in the Marshall Islands, passing close by Johnston Atoll. From Majuro we would sail west-southwest 782 miles to Ponape in the Federated States of Micronesia. Then we would sail west-northwest 980 miles to Saipan in the Northern Marianas.

The first week at sea was pretty uneventful other than the usual sorting out of things like fixing the regulator on the charging system, and an overheating problem on the engine.

We passed Johnston Atoll on Day six. It's a military island and is a hazardous waste disposal site. We had heard rumors that they incinerate our stockpiles of nerve gas here. As we passed by, Island Control came up on the radio, and wanted to know who we were, and what we were doing there. We told them, and they said to keep our distance. I had images of us all dying horrible deaths from nerve gas exposure as we passed by.

We caught two nice skipjack tuna as we passed the reef. We pondered whether or not we should eat them, considering the nature of the island. Hunger won out, and we had great sashimi and a delicious tuna dinner.

On the fourteenth night out, we noticed the lumen of Majuro from about fifty miles out. In the morning we entered the atoll. It's a good thing we waited for daylight, because the entrance wasn't anything like the chart. The buoys had all been changed to lights on poles, and the colors reversed to the international system with red on the left while entering. And the aero beacon at the airport had been moved to the new airport about five miles away.

Majuro lagoon is very large and beautiful. We had to travel about twelve miles across it to reach the main port of Olga, where we tied up at the main pier and went looking for port authorities to check us in. It turned out that it was National Fisherman's Day, and everyone was out fishing in a tournament, including the customs and immigration people. So we waited at the dock and drank beer with the tournament officials.

Majuro is a strange island. It was used as a base for U.S. planes during the Second World War. We kind of took it over, and have been compensating the islanders ever since for the use of the island, and for the people displaced from Bikini Atoll during the atomic bomb testing.

The United States connected several small islands of the atoll with a 32-mile long paved road. The inhabited part of the atoll is this 32-mile length, but it is only fifty feet to a quarter-mile wide, and 25,000 people live on this narrow strip of land.

Majuro is an example of U.S. civilization gone awry. The island is covered with stuff. Rusting military equipment, rusting heavy construction equipment, and rusty cars and trucks litter the scenery. The first thing that struck me is the number of cars and taxis. There is one paved road, and hundreds and hundreds of cars. You have to wait several minutes to cross the one street!

The Majorans get regular payments from the United States, and they don't have anything to spend it on, so they buy cars, and drive up and down the thirty-two-mile road.

The United States has changed the landscape on Majuro, but not the people. Everyone I met had a friendly smile and demeanor, and they went out of their way to make us feel comfortable and welcome. We were invited to the Fishing Tournament Picnic on one of the uninhabited islands. It was right out of a South Seas paradise poster. We swam and snorkeled in crystal-clear water among brightly colored tropical fish. I felt like I was in an aquarium. Then we joined the Marshallese for barbequed marlin, beer, music, dancing, and a lot of fish stories.

Carpe Diem anchored in Majuro Lagoon

Richie left us in Majuro and flew to Fiji to go surfing. We were joined by our three new crewmembers; Ben Bland from Maui, Steve Soenke from Saipan, and Rex and Clarie's nine-year old son, Nick.

The next day we cleared customs and immigration and cast off. It was evening, and as we motored across the lagoon, with all the homes lit up, it seemed we were surrounded by a ring of sparkling jewels.

The 780-mile passage from Majuro to Ponape took us from the Marshall Islands Republic to the Federated States of Micronesia. It was an uneventful crossing, with very light and variable winds all the way. We did a lot of motoring. It was very hot and humid with a lot of rain squalls and even some thunder and lightning.

Ponape appeared out of the rain on the sixth day. It was quite a different landfall than Majuro. It was a high volcanic island covered in vegetation, but it had a fringing reef.

The chart of the island was once again completely wrong. Like Majuro, the buoys had been replaced with beacons, and the lights had been reversed to the International System.

We negotiated the channel just before dark and found no room at the commercial dock, so we continued on up the lagoon and found good anchorage off the Kapingamarangi Village in Kolonia. The boat looked tiny moored under the towering Jokaj Rock.

Where Majuro was crowded, cluttered, and overrun with cars, Ponape was just the opposite. The high mountains are covered with tropical rain forests and waterfalls. Much of the island is uninhabited and untouched. It is a tropical paradise, abundant with coconut, breadfruit, and banana trees. The Ponapeans seem to be a happy, healthy, smiling group of people.

Ben left the boat in Ponape to get back to his job as a fireman on Maui. We gained a new crewperson, Vanessa, the Kosacks ten year old daughter, whom they adopted from Ponape.

Ponape

I got off the boat for a couple days to give the Kosack family some privacy. I checked into the Village Hotel, which is well worth a visit if you are ever in Ponape. Bob and Patti Arthur built a local-style hotel of thatched-roof bungalows nestled on a hillside in a tropical rain forest overlooking the ocean. The bungalows are simple, with ceiling fans, waterbeds, and unbelievable views.

During our stay in Ponape, we visited the Cultural Center, where we enjoyed the local music and dancing. We tasted the local drink, sekal, which is a narcotic similar to kava. We spent a day snorkeling on the reef and swimming in waterfalls. We also visited the ancient ruins of Nan Madol, a city of temples and canals built of basalt logs a thousand years ago.

I was glad to leave the "madness" of Majuro, but I could have lingered in Ponape. We had a boat to deliver, so we said good bye to "Paradise." We left Kolonia, motored through the reef, and headed northwest for Saipan, 880 miles away.

We passed close by the small atoll of Pakin in the evening and saw thousands of birds diving in the water and feeding. We put out a fishing line, and immediately caught a ten pound skipjack tuna. We enjoyed our first evening at sea with a fresh fish dinner and a beautiful sunset.

The winds filled in from the Northwest, and we had moderately strong trade winds of twelve to eighteen knots for the next several days. It was a delightful passage on a beam reach with sunny skies and starry nights. Clarie got seasick, but the kids, Vanessa and Nick, were fine. Vanessa slept with her eyes open—very strange! I wonder if it is a Ponapean trait.

We now had a crew of four adults and two children. Rex, Steve and I stood watches, three hours on and six hours off, Clarie cooked and stood watch when she felt like it, and the two kids stood watch with whomever they felt like. The adults kept themselves busy working on the engine, generator, water maker; We also occupied ourselves with navigating, steering, cooking, reading, and writing. The kids kept busy reading, writing in their journals, and playing cards, checkers, and chess.

As we neared the island of Saipan, we crossed the Mariana Trench. It is the deepest area of ocean on Earth, 5,000 fathoms (30,000 feet) deep. We couldn't resist temptation to stop and go for a swim. So we took down sails, put down the boarding ladder, and dove into the world's deepest swimming hole.

As we approached Saipan, I reread the Pilot for the area, and it said, "In the western part of Micronesia, typhoons are common and can occur the year round, but more often in the summer. The typhoons often form south of the Mariana Islands, and occasionally pass over Guam and Saipan with heavy rainfall and winds up to 200 mph." It was summer, and we were heading into Saipan! Needless to say, I was keeping a constant watch on the weather reports.

We sighted Saipan from quite a way off. It is a high volcanic island, and quite green. We had a pleasant sail in, and tied up at the new Smiling

Cove Marina just north of the commercial pier. We went through customs, and then drove to the Kosacks house.

Rex and Clarie were wonderful hosts, and I spent a couple delightful days sightseeing before I had to fly to Honolulu for the Kenwood Cup.

Saipan was the last big island battleground of World War II. Just one month before the end of the war, the Japanese defenders of Saipan moved their surviving forces to the northern end of the island for a suicidal last-ditch stand. As the Allied Forces moved in, hundreds of Japanese soldiers leapt to their deaths off the cliff. We visited their last command post, a series of caves dug into the mountainside. There were still Japanese cannons and artifacts in place. It was quite eerie.

Sightseeing in Saipan

Nineteen

Ragtime –
Transpac 1997

"Transpac Tale: Alone Together on Swift Wood."

*By John Balzar © Copyright, 1993, Los Angeles Times.
Reprinted with permission.*

Aboard the racing yacht *Ragtime,* in the Eastern Pacific—The night is moonless, and under layers of clouds also starless. The night is black—up, down, behind and beyond.

Into this darkness we race. Surely on a night like this the cliché was born—about racing like the wind. For the wind shrieks in our rigging, fills the oversize billows of our sails and sweeps us across the ocean. What we cannot see we feel: the pressure of breeze on our necks, the epic and unstable power of sea underfoot, spray in our faces, the boiling rush of the boat's wake. Over the turbulent Pacific we race like the wind.

Again and again, the classic 1963 sloop *Ragtime* points her snout and dives down the face of unseen waves, hesitating just a beat as the swell rises. Then her thin hull shivers and drops like a runaway elevator. Then we are racing faster than the wind.

Overleaf: Ragtime under sail.

We are surfing at 30 miles an hour into the night of the open ocean in a 65-foot sailboat, a single-masted wooden yacht with the profile of a carving knife and ghosts of legend in her past. Our pursuit is old and proud, and romanticized along waterfronts around the world. We are, of course, exuberant and as keenly alive as it is possible to be.

To the south, an ominous hurricane is blowing our way. Behind us is California and months of preparation. Ahead, if we make it, lies Hawaii and reunions with our families, strings of flower leis, iced jugs of mai tais and rounds of parties to celebrate one of America's most venerable sporting endeavors: the biannual Transpacific Yacht Race from Los Angeles to Honolulu. No ocean race in the world is so long and so old. Few are as exquisite. None takes sailors this far from land.

Sometimes the smear of stereotype obscures the grace, subtlety and drama of ocean racing. Rich people at play with expensive toys, arcane rules and clubhouse protests. But up close, competitive blue-water sailing satisfies more than its offhand image. For one thing, not all of the wealthy who sail are spoiled as sportsmen. A boat, no matter how big, is too small to hide unearned arrogance.

In truth, most of the people who sail the Transpac are not wealthy. They hold down jobs. This is their vacation, or for a few, their avocation. As kids, they played in dinghies. As adults, well, they never entirely grew up, except to look longingly at the horizon, to sail more skillfully and come to understand that every well-heeled fellow headed to sea needs crew. No one sails Transpac alone.

Aboard *Ragtime*, we sail with nine. All are volunteers and everyone works for a living: the boat's new owner; seven accomplished racing sailors, some of them greatly accomplished, and me, an eager coastal cruiser whose only potential asset is as storyteller. Nearly all of the 2,223-mile event occurs over the horizon and out of sight. Thus the great race is hardly fathomed inland of the wharves. It is an adventure recounted mostly at the salty bars of yacht clubs and in the pages of specialty magazines, with only stray news accounts here and there.

With degrees of pity and condescension these sailors regard those who do not appreciate the experience: this blend of graceful mechanism, human competition, and the immutable forces of nature.

"Out here life boils down to its simplest," says navigator John Jourdane, 53, a Pasadena schoolteacher who has twice raced around the world and made 32 previous Pacific crossings. "Out here you have only two things to worry about: making the boat go fast and what's for dinner.

"It's a simple life. It's peaceful. It's exciting. It's you, the ocean and your mates. All the other stuff, you leave behind. And one other thing, out here is one of the last great unspoiled wildernesses on the planet. Here, it's us and nature. Nobody can help us."

Pushing the Boat with Unceasing Effort

To drive a sailboat to its limits is unceasing effort. This is not a cruise. There is no cocktail hour, not a single chair in which to sit, no table around which to gather. The cabin below is smaller than a camping trailer, wide open and piled deep with bags of sails. It is sodden and rank like a gym locker. There is no shower. Duty watches pass, four hours on and five hours off, around the clock.

On deck, everything is sharp or hard, or both. The boat rolls and pitches spasmodically. One does not walk so much as climb from place to place. Anybody's stationary neck, shoulder, waist or knee is regarded as a communal hand-hold. There is no shade from the sun, no light against the dark save the faintest glow of instruments.

So how can we make the boat go fast? We can pick the right course, which in Transpac is a matter of understanding—and more important anticipating—ocean weather, that is, the variable breezes that whirl clockwise around the Eastern Pacific's summer high-pressure zone. In long-distance sailing, the fastest line between two points is seldom straight.

We can pick the right combination of sails according to the wind. *Ragtime* carries 16 for this race, including six giant, balloon-like spinnakers of various dimensions and weights, some for heavy air and others for light zephyrs.

We can leave behind unnecessary cargo. We bring only one tube of toothpaste to share, one can of deodorant. We daub our cuts and scrapes from the same little bottle of peroxide. We are limited to four T-shirts, two pairs of shorts, a sweater and foul-weather gear.

Each of us is permitted a personal toothbrush. But someone seems to have forgotten, and right now I see mine in the mouth of an off-watch colleague. Oh well, I am wearing another's jacket, which looked a lot like mine in the dark.

As is custom, the boat's owner has provided us with identical crew T-shirts, nylon jackets and ball caps. Some aboard mark theirs with initials. Others regard this as possessiveness and wear whatever is closest at hand.

To balance the boat, we keep our weight on the high side—the side from which the wind is coming, the weather side. We sleep in our clothes, ready to be summoned on deck. The entire trip, I never remove my contact lenses. We share pillows, soggy sheets and bunks still warm from the last body.

Inside, *Ragtime* is a noisy echo chamber for the roil of the sea, the humming of the rigging, the thud of footsteps on deck and screech of mechanical winches. No matter, we sleep, exhausted—if sometimes only for minutes before the call "All Hands!" to change a sail or course.

On deck, each standing watch of four people will bring us an average 46 to 51 miles closer to Hawaii. How much closer depends on the wind. But by no means the wind alone. No amount of advance reading or dockside conversation had prepared me for the physical effort and coordinated artistry necessary to gain the most from the breeze.

Seasickness Fells the Storyteller

Preparing for this voyage dockside, I had hoisted our enthusiastic 34-year-old bowman, Mike Burch, a Long Beach steamship agent, up *Ragtime*'s spindly 70-foot mast, using rope and winch. Suddenly a falling piece of rigging bounced off my head. I wavered and saw an explosion of stars.

"Lucky that was titanium and not stainless steel," someone remarked. So considering this standard of sympathy, I am not surprised to find myself being deployed as a floor mat 30 hours into the race.

You see, I am seasick; ghastly so. Curled up in the bilge, on wet bags of sails, inert, morose and full of self-doubt. I awaken, my stomach greasy and adrift from its moorings. Down here, I see a forest of hairy legs. The off watch is eating dinner. They are sitting on bunks. I am lying at their feet. Grinning mouths leer down. Crumbs or drips or something rain on me. The boat is pitching horribly. Hey, what about some pity? "OK," mutters Mike Burch. "We'll bake you a cake just as soon as the sea smoothes out a little." Someone else reminds me that no one dies of seasickness. We exchange profanities. I resume my position as floor mat.

During the six months I worked to earn a spot on the crew, I raced twice in *Ragtime*. Once to Mexico and once locally. I felt no queasiness and put the matter out of mind. But in the final ten days before Transpac, it seemed that everyone I met asked how sick I become in the big swells offshore. I began to dwell on the subject.

Two days before the start, I took meclizine tablets as suggested by a doctor. I stopped drinking alcohol and I ate nothing with grease or fat. Still, I could not shake the dread.

On race day, Saturday, July 5, we have a dockside goodbye party with family and friends. *Ragtime*'s small diesel engine propels us two hours from Long Beach to the starting buoy off Point Fermin.

Long ago, natural disaster fixed this place as our starting line. King Kalakaua of the independent monarchy of Hawaii got yachtsmen thinking in 1886 when he proposed a cross-Pacific sailboat race. In 1905, two boat owners, one from Honolulu and one from Los Angeles, agreed to race the following year. They decided the race should begin from San Francisco.

Hawaiian Clarence MacFarland arrived with his yacht La Paloma in May 1906 to find the city in ruins from the great earthquake and fire. The commodore of what is now the Los Angeles Yacht Club proposed moving the race south. It has been run from Southern California every other year except during world wars, and once during the Depression, the race was put off for a year. Among ocean races, only the Newport, RI.-to-Bermuda regatta is equally as old, but barely one-third the distance.

Before the starting gun, our last order of business is a crew meeting. John Jourdane, who has sailed 200,000 ocean miles, says this: "Any little scraps between us we left at the dock. We've got to be a family. This is our little world. There will be tension in the days ahead. Work it out."

We assign ourselves emergency duties. If the boat sinks I am to grab our "abandon ship" bag, which contains a satellite SOS transmitter. Two men are assigned life raft duties. Another is to gather our emergency jugs of water. "What's out there can be pretty scary," says Kevin McCarthy, a 36-year-old former professional sailor from Signal Hill. He adds: "But we've all been around the block. We can handle it." Wait, I think to myself, I've never been around this block.

We have a spectacular start. From our vantage, we lead the fleet. Under broken skies, the breeze is light and we ghost along toward the only marker on the course, the west end of Catalina. To stare out at the sea is as mesmerizing as looking into a campfire. I feel I am embarking on a timeless human ritual—an ocean passage in a small boat. For a change, I am on the other side of the press barrier. There is a helicopter overhead, and a couple of launches with photographers. A small fleet of spectator boats surrounds us.

Opposite: Ragtime rounding West End Catalina

As we round Catalina, the breeze is fitful. We change sails now and again. Small headsails when the wind puffs up. Larger sails when it dies down. We have dropped to last place among the seven boats in our class. It's early yet and *Ragtime* is never fast in these coastal conditions.

The spectator fleet is long gone. Our fellow racers are dispersing, picking their own courses, shrinking to little specks and vanishing over the horizon.

I wolf down a dinner of lasagna. Our boat has been provisioned by an outside professional. Each night's meal is packaged and designed to be heated on our small, gimbaled propane range and stove. The food is delicious, and prodigious. Even 100 miles offshore, we can detect the glow from the lights of Los Angeles. To the south, unseen, passes San Clemente Island, the last land for 2,100 miles.

Before my first night watch, I rest in a cramped single bunk deep in the stern of the boat. The breeze is growing stronger and the crash-bang of waves against the hull and the rush-gurgle of water inches from my ear are a lullaby. I wake sweaty, claustrophobic. Sick. For the next 32 hours I am immobilized, humiliated.

I am letting down the crew. They are doing my work, standing my watches. They took a chance on me, and I've spoiled things. I see the headline: Writer bites off more than he can chew and throws up. Then, in anger I think to hell with this boat and everyone on it. How can I endure another week of this? What doesn't kill you will make you stronger. Someone clever once said that. I spit in that person's eye.

Then the curse vanishes. I emerge from a sleep to find myself reborn at sea. I thank my mates for tolerating me. Which they regard as bizarre as my yearning for sympathy. The best single characteristic of sailors, at least these sailors, is the straight-ahead willingness to cope with whatever happens, without fretting about what might have been. The only thing sailors cannot abide is the absence of wind. Seasickness is part of sailing. I am to learn that more than half of first-time Transpac sailors get ill. And two others on our crew have also been queasy, unknown to me.

Before our voyage is over, I will celebrate and let the crew hoist me halfway up the great swaying mast while underway, just for the sheer joy of it.

Seeking Out the Trade Winds

Like most races, Transpac follows something of an established course. It is marked by the isobars of barometric pressure on the weather map. That's because a vast bubble of high pressure roves around the Eastern Pacific each summer. At the center of the bubble, the sea is typically flat and the air calm. The direct route from Los Angeles to Honolulu risks leading into this windless abyss, and certain defeat.

However, around the bubble, in a vast circle 2,000 miles in diameter, winds travel clockwise. They brush the West Coast of the United States with a prevailing northerly breeze and then bend and aim west—the fabled Trade Winds of the tropics. These breezes are fastest wherever pressure gradients are greatest, where the isobars squeeze close together. The job of navigator is to anticipate these winds and the swells that track them. This sends our fleet edging southward after Catalina. We turn more southerly than others.

Despite a slow start, the 1997 Transpac will turn out to be the windiest in decades. The fastest in history. Casualties in terms of broken boats and ruined dreams will be the greatest in a generation. Thirty-eight boats will start in various classes. Eight will retire, three of them dismasted, and one because of acute seasickness among the crew.

Because of weather patterns, Transpac is really two contests back to back. Leaving California, racers first sail into the wind and against the seas. Sailboats are pressed, or heeled, onto their sides. They bounce and slam into waves. This may make for exciting sailing for an afternoon off the coast, but sustained at sea, it becomes cold, wet, disorienting and uncomfortable. For hours on end, the off-watch crew sits on the high-side rail, legs dangling over the side, acting as counterbalance. Many sailors sew foam pads into the seats of their shorts for this duty.

Then hour by hour, day by day, the winds clock around to the stern. When they reach far enough behind, the ordinary jib or headsail is dropped and a giant spinnaker hoisted. The boat stands up straight. We are sailing downwind. The seas come from over our shoulder, and we can surf. Meanwhile, with each day the water and weather get warmer, more pleasant. It is this portion of the race that delights the sailors. It is the pattern of bad to good to great that makes the Transpac a standout in ocean racing.

Gentlemen, they say, prefer to sail downwind.

Not only is this more comfortable, but it is finesse sailing. Because we are now surfing and the giant spinnaker is an almighty challenge to fly under these conditions.

Traveling downwind, sails are no longer airfoils driving the boat forward like the wings of an airplane. They are wind-catchers, pulling us along. So that means the bigger sails the better—right up to the breaking point. Our primary spinnaker, made of a plastic-coated nylon as thin as tissue paper, is 66 feet tall and 44 feet wide, and balloons out larger than the floor plan of an average house.

I mentioned the artistry of ocean racing. And it is this: keeping ourselves moving at maximum speed toward Hawaii in a boat that wallows and slides over heaving seas in front of shifting winds, always right on the edge of a disastrous wreck. From above, our minute-by-minute course would appear as a zigzag. We veer to the left a little to surf the face of wave, then back to the right so we do not stall in the trough. Then we nudge back to the middle to set up for the next swell. Then the wind shifts a little and the whole ballet must shift with it.

When the breeze lightens, catching waves is harder. When the wind kicks in, surfing is more dangerous.

Essential to speed, of course, is technology—the ultra-expensive components and futuristic laboratory designs of modern sailing craft. However, as we will prove in this boat built when John F. Kennedy was president and Sonny Liston heavyweight boxing champion, the skill of the sailor remains decisive.

At the top of the wave, the spinnaker rides far forward and is taut with wind. But *Ragtime* outraces the wind when surfing. With no pressure on the spinnaker, the sail begins to collapse. The crew responds by reeling in one corner, tightening it again. Then it is released slowly as it fills. From above, the spinnaker would appear to breathe in and out.

Down in the cockpit, one person is directing the "trim" of the spinnaker and looking behind for the endless shifts and puffs in the ocean breeze. Another, the grinder, is bent over a two-handed winch, reeling in the spinnaker and then resting a moment before reeling in again. Another person is adjusting the winged-out mainsail for maximum drive, and perhaps also an optional sail flying between the forward spinnaker and the mast, called a staysail. The final member of the watch is at the helm, driving.

This, I quickly understand, is not like steering a cruising boat. Sitting at a traffic light in your car, imagine a 20-mph breeze coming from behind. That is the "actual" wind over the ground. As soon as you drive forward, however, the wind touching the car changes in velocity. When you are going 20 mph, you feel no breeze at all because you are traveling with it. When you reach 30 mph, you are driving into a 10-mph head wind. This is called "apparent" wind. This is what hits us when we accelerate down the face of a wave.

Helmsman and sail trimmers feel every shift on the hairs of their necks, verified by instruments on the mast. By that and the undulations of an agitated sea, the 25,000-pound boat is alternately sailed and surfed.

"If you are feeling old, come out here sailing. This will bring you to life," says Bruce McPherson, 40, a Seattle yacht broker and native New Zealander who spent 17 years as a professional sailor on the world's maxi boat series.

The price of speed is danger. If the boat veers even slightly out of this groove, the wind will catch us sideways and we are likely to be knocked down. *Ragtime* will "crash" or broach—perhaps plunging the rigging into a wave and breaking the mast. A driver lasts only an hour at a time before his concentration begins to go.

At night or in high winds, the challenge is far greater. At these moments, the eyes behind the helm narrow and hands twirl the four-foot spoked wheel at a blurring pace. It is a fierce and unforgiving experience—and for those who can accomplish it, sublime.

Hurricane Headed Toward Ragtime

It is afternoon now, our third day at sea. John Jourdane comes on deck after studying the latest of our twice-a-day weather faxes.

"There's a full-blown hurricane 800 miles away coming right for us," he announces. "We'll watch it, but usually these things dissipate when they reach cooler water up here." Usually? Our contact with the outside world is through these broadcast faxes, and a once-a-morning sideband radio check-in with the Transpac race committee which is traveling the course with us in a communications sailboat. We have not seen another vessel since Catalina Island, and these position check-ins allow us to learn how the race is progressing.

We are still seventh of seven boats in our class, and 20th of 23 racing boats in the fleet. The remaining vessels are slower and are competing in a new "cruising" class.

"Don't be discouraged," Jourdane says. "*Ragtime* hasn't seen her stuff yet." Her "stuff" will come in the downwind portion of the race where the 34-year-old boat remains as fast as any its size.

All of the large race boats in Transpac, in fact, owe a debt to *Ragtime*. When she arrived in California from New Zealand, the low-slung stream-liner was an oddity. Oceangoing racers were supposed to be big, sturdy craft. *Ragtime* was an eggshell by comparison.

Ragtime's "spacious" navigation station with no seat

She was designed light—to surf downwind and nothing else. Yacht club regulars barred her from racing because she was so fragile.

Finally, in 1973, *Ragtime* premiered in the Transpac. In the last 50 miles, she edged out a larger, heavier boat that was the odds-on favorite. A headline in *The Times* recorded it as, "The Time a 'Rowboat' Beat the 'Queen Mary.'" West Coast racing was changed forever. *Ragtime* signaled the era of the Ultra-Light Displacement Boat, ULDB, which subsequently gave rise to a series of boats designed specifically for Transpac—craft three feet longer than *Ragtime*, and much wider than her needle-sized, 9 1/2-foot beam. But all had the similar ability to surf. These boats are called "sleds" and it is against this new generation that *Ragtime* now races.

A handful of these craft were modified to add more height to their masts and more lead to their keels for 1997 to establish a separate and still faster class, known as the "turbo sleds." They will gain 20 to 30 miles a day on us and shatter all race records. Until then *Ragtime* could claim three of the fastest 25 crossings in race history.

The Transpac now underway is *Ragtime's* 11th, and she's hardly slowing down. At the finish, we will have shaved four minutes and 43 seconds off her previous best.

One Log Can Ruin Your Whole Voyage

"Holy cow! Look at that! Gosh!" Actually, crewman Ty Pryne, 39, a Honolulu sailboat rigger, put it slightly differently. Sailors, you see, tend to leave their manners ashore. In this case, Pryne is pointing to a large log drifting 75 feet off our beam. We whisk past the ominous tree floating out here hundreds of miles from land, and other crewmen voice their version of "Holy Cow!"

One of the ocean racer's gravest fears is colliding with a heavy, half-submerged object and tearing a fatal hole in the thin plywood hull. Worse than logs are sleeping whales and sodden shipping containers that have washed off freighters and float only inches above the surface. These could easily peel away *Ragtime*'s stabilizing keel and much of her bottom, sending us down almost instantly.

Even in daylight, it is difficult to see such objects, particularly because everyone's concentration is fixed on the wind behind us and the sails overhead. At night, seeing anything smaller than a well-lit freighter is impossible.

For this reason, we sleep with our feet forward in the bunks as shock absorbers in a collision. Nothing else to do, except tell ourselves that it is a big ocean and stray obstacles and dozing whales are comparatively few. But whenever I lie down, I visualize in my mind how many steps in the dark it is to the "abandon-ship" bag, which is my emergency responsibility. I try to push out of mind the stories of sailors swimming through battery acid in an upturned boat, groping for a way out. I try to forget reading that the average depth of the Pacific is 13,215 feet.

In 1975, a small Transpac boat sunk suddenly in the middle of the race. Its crew of six was rescued by another competitor.

More absorbing, certainly for me, is the fear of being washed overboard and lost. Not a matter of chance, like hitting a container, but a personal screw-up, a momentary loss of concentration, a single missed handhold. I imagine the shocking sensation of wetness, the choking in my throat, so I cannot even try to yell at the pyramid of sail vanishing over the swells. Then the aloneness.

The velocity at which we are traveling, and more to the point, the sensation of velocity aboard such a boat, is a steady reminder of this hazard. It is also the source of excitement, for isn't exhilaration the blood offspring of fear? Our bow sometimes raises a thundering wake eight feet high, knifing through swells, and our stern kicks up a rooster tail worthy of a ski boat. Even after I become accustomed to everything else aboard—the rituals of the work, the cramped quarters, the open toilet an arm's length from someone's sleeping bunk—after all that becomes familiar, the impression of speed, the rushing watery howling noise of speed, is still breathtaking.

Repeatedly, I find myself transfixed watching bits of foam from our bow wake race past the hull and disappear behind us, over the swells in just seconds. A student of Zen once told me about Tokyo businessmen who stand at the edge of the platform just as the commuter train screeches into the station. By realizing that only a fraction of an inch separates them from tumbling to a crushing death, they face the day with a freshly aroused passion for life. I watch the foam vanish, and my heart rate rises.

I calculate that if it took the crew just five minutes to recognize that one of us is missing and drop giant spinnaker and bring *Ragtime* to a halt, 1.5 miles may separate swimmer from boat: surely an impossible distance to see a tiny bobbing head or waving hand in heavy seas, even if the sun is out.

In 1951, a Transpac boat suffered just such a calamity. The search was called off after 29 hours. Only then did a returning rescue boat chance upon the swimming crewman, who was brought aboard terrified but otherwise all right.

Howling Winds, a Ripple of Panic

By Day 4, we have moved up to sixth out of seven among the sleds. For dinner, enchiladas.

On Day 5, we break a magic barrier in ocean racing: we have traveled 307 miles in the last 24 hours. Hurricane Delores, downgraded to a tropical storm, has moved into the neighborhood, 300 miles away, and still coming our way. We can detect nothing of it, but no one is joking or telling ghost stories about storms at sea. Dinner: turkey and dressing.

At night, the winds howl. A ripple of panic disrupts my watch. Scott Zimmer, the imposing 6-foot-5, 37-year-old owner of *Ragtime*, is a coastal racer with most of his experience in small boats. This is his inaugural ocean passage, and his first night at the helm under these conditions. He lasts only moments.

"Take this. Here, take it!" He steps back from the wheel like a man whose hands have been scorched.

It takes awhile for another helmsman to restore something approaching confidence in the watch. None of the more experienced racers think anything less of Zimmer, and some admire his moxie for trying. This is one of sailing's greatest challenges, and Zimmer is as surprised as I am by the dexterity necessary to keep us from calamity. He won't smile about it for a couple of days.

On Day 6, we advance to fourth place in our class, and seventh in the fleet. Our mood soars because we expect winds for the remainder of the race to favor *Ragtime*. And more important, we are in a southerly position where we can best capitalize on the weather for our approach to the islands. We begin to dream of a miracle.

At midday we see a dot on the horizon. It is a spinnaker headed our way. The sled *Grand Illusion* has shifted course and is bearing down. She will cross behind us after falling back in a brief mid-ocean duel. She is heading farther south still, a fact we disregard.

That may have been our downfall. Our weather fax has been acting up, so we're 12 hours behind the latest forecast. It appears that *Grand Illusion* could see on the map that remnants of Delores had altered the prevailing position of the strongest winds.

None of us pay any mind. I am trying to put to words the feeling of space on the open ocean. What I anticipated was an overwhelming sensation of vastness. I find just the opposite. I am astounded how small our world has become. Only in the abstract are we part of that great expansive arc from horizon to horizon and the empty leagues beyond. Our world is bounded by wood and sailcloth. I go aloft into the rigging and *Ragtime* seems even more preposterously dwarfish.

In this shrunken space, we are acutely aware of being alone. We know that other racers are on our flanks beyond the curve of the earth but otherwise, this part of the ocean is as vacant as it's been since the advent of the steamship. That is to say, almost no one hunts for the wind here now, except occasional sailboats like us. Freighters follow more direct lanes. Airline routes go elsewhere. We have seen not a single plane.

Twice, porpoise give chase and then drift away. Occasionally pelagic birds pay a visit, including one lanky albatross. At night, flying fish sometimes mistakenly land on our decks with a thud and rattle. Once in a while, squid break the surface to escape predators.

The ocean is a richer, viscous blue now. We are in the Trade Winds. The horizon is darkened by rainsqualls. We try to use these mini-storms to our advantage—seeking out their winds, but bearing away to avoid the large calms that follow in their wake. Their drizzle and rain is refreshing, and washes off the itch of salt scum.

In the heat of day, we strip one by one and scrub ourselves in salt water on the fantail of the boat. We are allotted a quart of precious fresh water each for a sponge rinse. We hang laundry from the lifelines and graceful *Ragtime* takes on the air of a scow.

A couple of the old hands surprise us by baking chocolate chip cookies. We have 800 miles to go. We dare to contemplate our finish. There is no liquor allowed on board, although I suspect that someone is bending the rule. The best the rest of us can do is dream of the mai tais that our hosts in Hawaii will have waiting for us. Tubs of them. No, make it barrels full.

Later, nightfall. The stars are marvelous. Not just bright, but three-dimensional in their profusion. We can see depth in the Milky Way. Starlight shimmers off the water. A sliver of moon appears and lights a direct path to Hawaii.

The Chemistry of a Crew

What's on your mind, Bruce? Bruce McPherson, the onetime professional racer, is the most colorful of our cast—with a rap sheet of ribald sailing antics known on several continents. He is also enough of a serious sailor to have worked on New Zealand's most recent America's Cup challenge and many of the great "maxi boats" of the day. Now he is quiet, and staring at me. "I'm just thinking how different we are," he replies. "I was born into this. For you it's all so strange." Yes, surely.

We are a small group confined in an even smaller space. Until this race, we have not sailed together. Yet, camaraderie is always high on the sailors' list of reasons for going to sea—a chance for the boys, or the girls, or sometimes the boys and girls, to escape social constraints and act and talk with freedom. That is, to carry on like sailors in ways that might not be acceptable, or comfortable, around the office water cooler.

A similar dynamic of interdependence and social release draws people together for all variety of adventures. At sea the difference is that escape is impossible. Even the 65-foot length of the boat is deceiving since the forward half is often awash in water.

McPherson has given up the full-time sailor's life for a family in the Pacific Northwest. He named his daughter Jennica after a sail known as the gennaker, and admits that his wife has quieted his wildness. After a few days at sea, he realizes that he misses this life deeply. His sailing is the most stylish of anyone's on the crew.

Our bowman, Mike Burch, is still rising in the ranks of West Coast sailors. During months of preparation, he shows himself a doting father. In a chase boat, Burch's family follows *Ragtime* for nearly an hour at the start of the race, waving and yelling encouragement the whole time. They will be the first voices we hear from the dock in Honolulu.

A couple of times a day, no matter what conditions, he is hoisted aloft to check the rigging. His body is deeply bruised from the beating he takes aloft. But he insists on standing extra watches because he cannot sleep from excitement.

Kevin McCarthy also was a professional racing yachtsman with an impressive resume. He, too, has gone ashore to build a more normal life as a manager for a mechanical engineering firm. He is steady, unflappable, a patient teacher and can rally the crew. He's our best man in the galley, and as a sailor he is that rare combination of being both gifted and rock solid.

John Jourdane is our leader, a proud, unassuming, non-confrontational master of this craft. We all gaze up to him. If another helmsman can push us up to 12 knots (a nautical mile being 15% greater than a statute mile), Jourdane draws his lips into a scowl and advances us to 12.5. He is the author of the book "Icebergs Port and Starboard," about his 33,000-mile Whitbread race around the world in 1989–90. He could command a berth on most of the boats in the Transpac. He chose *Ragtime* because "it's a legend. It's like being part of the Hall of Fame. Sailors all over Hawaii and California think of it as their boat. It's sailing history." Because of him, many of these other good sailors have joined this crew.

Another ex-professional sailor with us is John Norman—yes, there are three Johns on our crew, a source of endless confusion. We try to distinguish by using last names, initials, mothers' maiden names. Nothing seems to catch on. Finally we give up. If an order goes out for "John" to do something, we find that it gets done.

Norman is a 42-year-old construction development manager in Long Beach, a precise sailor with military bearing. He, more than anyone, inspires me to prove myself. He regards sailing as a high calling. He keeps the boat orderly and his watch mates focused.

Ty Pryne, the Hawaii rigger, is exuberant. This is his second Transpac race in *Ragtime.* Six years ago, he oversaw the last refit of the yacht and hardly anyone knows it better. Our watches overlap and I have never known anyone more at ease on the water. He is so deft you hardly notice him work.

Buddy Richley, 40, is a Newport Beach investment counselor and captain of his own 48-foot race boat. He is an athletic, disciplined sailor with a keen desire to win. This is his third Transpac and he jumped at the chance: "I'll be able to tell my kids I went to Hawaii on *Ragtime.*"

The most complicated character aboard is Scott Zimmer, who bought *Ragtime* last autumn for pennies on the dollar after the previous owner invested $1.5 million in overhauling the vessel. Zimmer manufactures advertising blimps in Huntington Beach, the kind tethered over automobile dealerships. He throws himself at every kind of competitive endeavor, from rowing to polo. He surfs, skis, flies and owes most of his sailing to the ultra-competitive 22-foot Star class.

He got the Transpac bug in 1991 and set himself a 10-year goal to make the race. It is a big leap, not only by the size of the boat but the dynamics of teamwork. He does not assume the role of skipper; his crew has 100 combined years of blue-water experience more than he does. But he is responsible, and he is the owner and the owner is owed deference.

In turns, Zimmer is open, charming and brims with enthusiasm, then becomes self-absorbed, testy and withdrawn. He sometimes works the ordinary rotation of jobs on watch, then asserts himself and practices his driving when it pleases him—forget the order of watches.

John Jourdane warned of tensions. They emerge between Zimmer and his crew. Small things, mostly, sparks from the colliding egos of the financier, who is sometimes referred to in his absence as "The Wallet," and sailors who feel they are being asked to both win and allow the owner his indulgences.

In the end, Zimmer and the bulk of his crew feel equally underappreciated. As navies found out centuries ago, leadership at sea is a unique burden. Some of the crew complain that Zimmer is spending too much time at the wheel chasing the biggest waves to surf without regard to maintaining our optimum course. Zimmer bristles and insists he is driving as well as anyone.

"You want to drive, you write the check," he snaps. Money is at the root of some of the friction. Zimmer worries often about the expense of the race, and deservedly so. One afternoon during preparations, I watch as he is presented with an accounting of $27,000 for sails, rigging, supplies and logistics. Some of the crew demands he spend still more even though several sponsorship leads evaporate in the months before the race. Only in the final weeks, a partnership of Santa Clara-based 3Com, a computer hardware manufacturer, and Ingram Micro, the large computer distributor based in Santa Ana, come forth enthusiastically.

All of us enjoy the irony of this: a classic craft flying the logos of 21st century technology companies. *Ragtime* again the futurist, and never mind the bickering.

In 5th Place but at Bad Wind Angle

Day 7. "Well, we took a punch. Now we go on and do the best we can. We didn't get the wind shift we planned on last night." John Jourdane has just finished the morning radio call-in. We are in fifth place, as measured by a straight line. But we no longer command the most favorable wind angle for our final turn toward Hawaii.

Our course has carried us first south of the direct rhumb line, and now north, following the flow of high-pressure winds. Now we are preparing to turn left and run directly to Oahu. But our weather fax did not pick up the forecast yesterday, so we are late in learning that remnants of Tropical Storm Delores now favor those boats that moved sooner.

All we can do is sail like maniacs. The sun is glaring hot. We sweat and concentrate and bite our lips. The trouble is, we know that nobody else is doing less. Dinner: spaghetti.

Day 8. We have lost our steady breeze. I check the electronic GPS, or global positioning system. This little satellite receiver tells me where I'm at within thirty feet or so anywhere on the planet. As it happens, I am 195 miles west-northwest from the red buoy off

Waikiki's Diamond Head, where the Transpac ends in one of the most picturesque settings in all of yachting.

My notebook says tempers are a bit raw, although it does not remind me why. Perhaps because we have run short of drinking water. We are down to a couple of small plastic bottles apiece. So naturally our thirst is unquenchable.

The horizon is empty still, but the morning radio-check confirms that the fleet of sleds, once spread over more than 100 miles of ocean, is converging in a bottleneck for the final run to the finish. As we could have predicted, we have fallen back to sixth place.

We gather for a pep talk, and vow to sail even harder than yesterday. We move everything that is not bolted down to the very center of the boat to balance it perfectly.

From our freezer, kept cold by running the engine two hours a day as we charge batteries, we thaw our final dinner of steak and lobster. Nature serves up dessert: a colossal tropical orange sunset behind a lineup of towering Trade Wind clouds. There is almost no chatter on watch, just anticipation.

Because we see no other boats, we are tempted one final time to dream. Race rules require boats to check in by radio when they are 100 miles from the finish. Then again at 25 miles. As we come closer to 100, we listen in for the calls of those ahead of us. The silence urges us on.

Then the calls come, and we know there will be no miracle finish. There are several boats ahead. Not far, but still ahead.

Then the first twinkle of lights on land, the island of Molokai. We dash down the famous Molokai channel, then past Koko Head and Diamond Head and the red buoy. There is a white explosion of television lights. The wind is almost completely dead when we drop sails and start the engine. It is nearly 4 o'clock Monday morning. We scurry to straighten up the boat and change into the clean shirt each of us has been saving.

Events become a blur. We approach the marina. The booming PA system at the Honolulu Yacht Club welcomes us with an "Aloha," and congratulates each crewman by name. We congratulate each other with slaps on the back and hugs and watery eyes.

Then there is an opening at the dock. My wife is waving. Mike Burch's kids are yelling. There are photographers and a sea of strangers. The Chart House restaurant, which has long been the host committee for *Ragtime*, has raised a tent in the parking lot. Here we find those coveted jugs of mai tais, which are hereafter named "Guy Tais" after bartender Guy Maynard.

Leis are piling around on my neck. No smell is more astonishing than tropical flowers after a stint at sea. Strange women keep kissing me. Men grab my hand. My legs feel spongy on the solid ground. Someone has put a cigar in my mouth. I have to turn away from the crowd and take a breath to keep from being overwhelmed. Hawaiians have always treated an ocean passage as an achievement.

I remember the soft break of dawn. And the first shafts of yellowish light on *Ragtime's* black hull, now quiet and harnessed to pilings. I remember we finished sixth out of seven. Our time: eight days, 17 hours, 46 minutes, 54 seconds—only two hours and 19 minutes behind the leader. I remember walking Waikiki with my mates, and the rounds of parties in the days that followed, and that childish food fight in a crowded restaurant. I remember being given a finisher's paperweight at the trophy dinner. I remember cleaning *Ragtime* one last time and taking supporters day sailing in the fresh Trade Winds off of Diamond Head.

I remember the handshakes and goodbyes. I remember the awkward, self-conscious farewell to old fleet-footed, sure-footed *Ragtime*, which now passes to other crews for new adventures. Best, of all, I remember my mates calling me "jig." That's the lowest form of sailor. But a sailor still. Fair winds.

John and Greta get married on Ragtime

The Surprise Wedding

After the Transpac Race in 1997, my girlfriend, Greta and I decided to get married. To make it unique, we planned to get married on *Ragtime* in Alamitos Bay near our little cottage in Naples.

Then to make it more interesting, we would have the *Ragtime* Transpac crew be our wedding party. The big difference from a normal wedding was that know one would know it was a wedding until they came aboard the boat. We only told three people about it, my brother, Mo, who is a judge and could marry us, and my best man Mark Donohue and Greta's maid of honor, Lisa Donohue, Mark's wife.

Scott Zimmer graciously lent me *Ragtime* to take the crew out for a "harbor cruise," and we invited all the crew to join us for an end of the summer harbor cruse and luau. Then we invited all our family to come to our house for an end-of-summer luau.

Greta's good friends Bertie and Red Forst shipped in fresh flower leis from Hawaii, and as the crew came aboard with their wives and girl friends, we gave each one a lei, and told them it wasn't a harbor cruise, but our wedding. We then sailed the boat across the bay to a small park in Naples, near our house, where our families were waiting, thinking we were just going to have a luau.

After the boat was tied up at the park, Greta and I went to the bow of the boat where Mo performed the wedding ceremony. We had written our own wedding vows, and they were passed out to all the family members, so they could follow along. Then we toasted with champagne, returned the boat to her slip, and then went to our little cottage, where we had rip-roaring wedding party on our front lawn. It was definitely a unique wedding, and one people still talk about.

Twenty

Magnitude
Magnitude—Andrews 70

Owner—Doug Baker
Crew—Rob Wallace, Steve Dodd, John Jourdane, Keith Kilpatrick,
Kevin McCarthy, Wally Gordon, Steve Cotton, Fred O'Connor,
Bill Meninger, Mike Van Dyke, Alan Harbour

The Channel Islands Race

In the spring of 1996, I was teaching at the Chandler School in Pasadena, California. Doug Baker called and asked if I would be interested in doing the Channel Islands Race on *Magnitude*, his new Andrews 70 turbo sled. Doug and I go way back. I raced with him to La Paz, Mexico, in 1978 on his Ericson 46, *Bacchus*, and then delivered the boat back to Long Beach. He's a great owner, who really enjoys sailing, and has a lot of fun.

We would be racing from San Pedro to Santa Barbara, then outside all the Islands off Southern California, and finish at San Pedro. It sounded like fun, although it can get pretty rough outside San Miguel and San Nicholas islands.

We started off Los Angeles Yacht Club, and sailed in light air around Palos Verdes and across Santa Monica Bay past Malibu. The wind slowly picked up as we passed Santa Barbara during the night. We beat out the Santa Barbara Channel in fifteen to twenty knots.

At first light as we rounded San Miguel Island, we set the big asymmetrical spinnaker. The boat took off and we were reaching along at 15 knots. The run from San Miguel to San Nicholas to San Clemente Island was very fast. We were surfing to twenty-five knots at times, and we were far ahead of the fleet and the course record.

As we sailed around the bottom of San Clemente Island, we set up to take down the spinnaker, and put up a jib. Alan Harbour took the fore guy, which was in a stopper, off the winch, to prepare it for the take down. Then the stopper let go and took Alan's hand with the line wrapped around it through the stopper. I was working at the navigation station below, when Alan came down the companionway ladder holding his hand. There was a lot of blood dripping. I said, "Alan, what's going on?" And he replied, "Big Problem," and collapsed on the cabin sole. I lifted his right hand off his left, and saw two stubs where fingers should have been.

Everyone was panicking, and Alan, a retired fireman, was the calmest man on the boat. He told me to stick his hand in a bowl of peroxide to kill the germs. Then wrap it with gauze and put it in a bag of ice. I wrapped it in gauze, but we didn't have any ice, so we used a bag of frozen vegetables. We held the hand up, with the frozen vegetables on it, and the bleeding stopped.

I sat with Alan, and kept talking with him, and taking his pulse to see if he was going into shock. Meanwhile Rob Wallace was on the radio talking to the Coast Guard. He informed them of the situation, gave our position, and they said to proceed to Pyramid Cove on San Clemente Island. A Coast Guard helicopter was on the way.

San Clemente Island is a Navy target island; the Navy came up on the radio and said we couldn't go into Pyramid Cove because it was a restricted area. We were looking at the cove, and there were two fishing boats and a sailboat at anchor, so we decided to listen to the Coast Guard and not the Navy. We anchored in the cove and waited for the helicopter. We took off the backstay, and supported the mast by leading the runners forward.

The helicopter arrived within a half hour from when we first made radio contact. It came in low, and downwash from the rotors was like a hurricane. The boat started swinging around the anchor, but the Coast Guard pilot was very good! They dropped the basket right on our after deck. We put Alan in the basket along with a Ziploc bag containing his two loose fingers, and they hauled him up. He arrived at Scripps Hospital in San Diego twenty minutes later.

Kudos to the Coast Guard! They are very good at what they do.

Pacific Cup – 1998

There was a biting cold wind flowing in through the Golden Gate as we started the race. Only five boats were in our start but they were all seventy to seventy-five feet in length; *Pyewacket*, *Zephyrus*, *Merlin*, *Rage*, and *Magnitude*. They were all circling around in the early morning fog, like sharks getting ready to attack.

We put up a #1 genoa, while the other boats put up #3 jibs. It paid off for us, and we did well leaving the bay. Jeff Madrigali, on *Zephyrus*, had a great start and jumped out ahead. But with our #1 genny, we were able to sail higher and faster than *Pyewacket*, *Merlin*, and *Rage*, and led them out them out under the Golden Gate Bridge.

It wasn't windy outside the Bay, but the seas were confused with the end of the ebb tide flowing against the wind. We were crossing the infamous Potato Patch. The wind did slowly build, and we changed to the #3 jib, and started reaching for our first waypoint.

It was a wild, wet first night with the wind building to thirty knots. We reached with the #3 on the rail, and it was a wet and fast ride.

Zephyrus did not report in at roll call the next morning. The wind and seas continued to build until we had steady thirty-knot winds and ten-foot seas. Luckily it kept veering to the north, coming aft, and the seas started lining up with the wind.

We changed to a jib top and genoa staysail, and were doing steady fifteen to sixteen knots of boat speed.

A couple crew were seasick the first night (probably too much partying in San Francisco), but they were coming around. We had six men on a watch, and only five bunks to weather, so one guy slept on the sails on the weather side.

The next day we set the small asymmetrical spinnaker, tacked to the bow, not the pole. We heard at roll call that *Zephyrus* had been dismasted the first night, and it was on its way back. It was too bad; they had lost their mast the previous year in Transpac, also.

Magnitude had also had mast problems the year before and had to return to Los Angeles. We were all keeping our fingers crossed, hoping our mast stayed up in this race.

We had made 320 miles in the second twenty-four hours; good speed, but the boat felt underpowered. We hoisted the next larger spinnaker, the A-3, which was set on the spinnaker pole, and was a lot larger. The boat said, "thank you," and took off. It was very easy to steer.

We had a dark night, full of rain squalls, and in the morning put up the A-2 spinnaker, which is considerably larger. And as soon as we got it up and filled, all hell broke loose. The fore guy block broke, the pole skied, the head of the chute blew out, and it dropped in the water. It filled with water, and by the time we got it back aboard, it was in pieces.

We set a small spinnaker, got settled, then changed to the big A-1. The boat started surfing very fast. Even with our problems, we did 337 miles in the third twenty-four hours.

It was Fred's fiftieth birthday, so we made him a birthday card out of a weather map, wrapped up a chocolate candy bar as a present, and sang

Happy Birthday.

The wind built, and we changed back to the A-3. The boat felt more in control with the smaller sail.

Alan Harbour had been the cook for the race, but since we lost him in the accident, we all took turns cooking. The food was no where near as good as when Alan cooked, but it was edible.

Our fourth day's run was 324 miles. We were getting down the course quickly, well ahead of *Rage*'s record of 7 days, 22 hours.

The wind came aft during the night, and we did a couple jibes. They were pretty rough, since we hadn't practiced doing them for quite a while. But nothing broke, and each jibe was smoother than the one before.

The fifth day's run was 329 miles, and the sixth was 320. We had put together quite an impressive run. This was a solid crew. Everyone aboard was a good helmsman.

The only problem was toilet paper. On the third day out, we discovered that we had only brought 4 rolls for 11 guys for 8 days. Someone's math was off when shopping for toilet paper. But we found that weather maps have another use besides predicting weather.

We broke the spinnaker pole during the last night while doing a jibe. We dropped the big spinnaker, and set the small A-3 tacked to the bow.

Kalaupapa Light on Molokai was sighted early in the morning, and we crossed the finish line at 8:30 AM. We were third to finish behind *Pyewacket* and *Merlin*.

It was a Transpacific race to remember; we covered over 300 miles every day, and sailed from San Francisco to Hawaii in 6 days, 23 hours!

Twenty-One

Kirawan –
Bermuda Race 2000
Kirawan – Rhodes 53-foot cutter

Owner—Sandy Horowitz
Crew—Tom Adams, John Jourdane, John Rousmanierre, Rick Peters

I received a call from Tom Adams in Marina del Rey asking me if I was interested in sailing an old wooden boat to Bermuda. I love *Ragtime*, an old wooden boat, so I asked for more information. He had been completely restoring *Kirawan*, a 1936 Phillip Rhodes design, and the boat was going to be trucked to Newport, Rhode Island, to race in the 2000 Newport to Bermuda Race. It sounded great, so I said yes.

Kirawan has a true pedigree. She is a 53-foot sloop, and won the Bermuda Race's coveted Lighthouse Trophy for first overall on corrected time in the 1936 race.

The boat was now owned by Sandy Horowitz, a movie producer in Hollywood, who loved old wooden boats. He was justifiably proud of the restored *Kirawan*.

Getting to Newport turned out to be the hardest part of the race. I flew from Los Angeles to Chicago, but when I arrived, there were tornado warnings up, and all flights were cancelled. The earliest flight to Connecticut was the next morning, so I checked all the hotels around the

SAILING WITH SCOUNDRELS AND KINGS

airport, and they were all sold out. All right, I thought, I will catch a taxi into downtown Chicago and get a hotel. So, I drove downtown, and every hotel was sold out. There was a national AFL-CIO convention going on. After my tenth rejection, I hopped in a taxi, and said, start driving toward O'Hare Airport, and stop at the first motel or hotel we see with a vacancy sign. Finally, about ten miles from the airport, we found a Holiday Inn with a vacancy.

I did fly out the next day, but barely made it to Newport in time to find the boat and Sandy, and ran to the Skipper's Meeting. We docked *Kirawan* at Elizabeth Meyer's International Yacht Restoration School, where she fit right in with all the beautiful restored wooden boats.

John Rousmanierre was on the crew, and I looked forward to sailing with him after reading all of his articles on seamanship over the years.

The following is excerpted from an article by John Rousmanierre about our race on *Kirawan*:

The race started out perfectly. We close-reached in 20-knot south-westerlies, which was just to *Kirawan's* liking. The boat sped along comfortably under a full moon.

We found some favorable eddies in the Gulf Stream, that gave us a couple more knots of boat speed, and were doing very well, covering over 200 miles each of the first two days. We were leading our class on the third morning.

Kirawan, the largest boat in the Classic Boat division, had pulled well ahead of her competitors in the breeze. The boat was in her element, fast and with an easy motion. Even in the hard reaching, with spray flying most of the time and solid water occasionally sweeping the decks, our crew of seven was able to sleep, eat, and move around relatively easily on the sturdy platform of the heavy displacement and long over-hangs. We were well prepared in gear, manpower, and spirit, yet there were some surprises.

The first night out, in a cold fog, we were shaken by the thunder of a powerful fog horn from a large commercial vessel that had stumbled into the middle of the race. Her crew, who must not have been keeping up with the Notice to Mariners, made their surprise and unhappiness known by horn and radio. When the Coast Guard instructed the captain to clear Channel 16 because he was not in an emergency situation, he testily replied that if looking at the radar and seeing 100 boats aimed at him was not an emergency, he did not know what was. A sailor interrupted him, and said, "You mean 176 boats." There were no collisions.

Tom Adams repairing Kirawan's sprung plank (photo by John Rousmaniere).

We reached fast into the second day, which brought an unusual sighting of an albino dolphin. Later we sailed into a large pod of more conventional dolphins, and a breaching whale.

Sitting at the navigator's station, John Jourdane felt a spray of water on his legs. Inspection revealed that a seam near the waterline on the windward side had opened up. Tom Adams, who had supervised the boat's refit, quickly devised a solution. A bosun's sling was hooked to a halyard and to two guy lines, one leading forward and the other aft. Wearing this combination safety harness/inflatable PF, Tom sat in the sling and, steadied by the guy lines, was lowered over the side to the seam, just above the water. Smacked regularly by waves, he methodically filled the gap with polysulfide sealant as we sailed on at six knots. After an hour of this strenuous work, Tom and inspectors inside the hull declared themselves satisfied with the repair.

We carried on with some trepidation, but no leaks, and as we entered the Bermuda high and the forces on the boat died, the planks sprang back into place, allowing us to sail confidently on port tack.

On the third day, the breeze faded to the teens, pulling the apparent wind forward and presenting a difficult tactical problem familiar to all sailors. With the wind now on the nose, should we sail high and slow, or low and fast? Our heavy boat needed speed, so we replaced the double-headsail rig (outer jib and forestaysail) with a big genoa and eased sheets a little. We were not alone. Many other boats cracked off from 30 degrees apparent wind to as much as 40 degrees. "Cheap speed," as this has been called, is a short term investment; distance lost to windward has to be made up in the future, and this time was no exception. As we sailed into the light air of the Bermuda High, the wind faded and backed into the south, imposing a long slow beat to the finish. We were reminded once again that the only objects that make much progress over the water in a five-knot headwind are sea birds and jet planes.

We finally finished off St. David's Lighthouse, then made the long motor inside the reefs to Hamilton and the Royal Bermuda Yacht Club, and several "Dark and Stormies" (a local drink of Goslings Black Seal Rum and ginger beer).

Twenty-Two

Medicine Man

Medicine Man — 61-foot Alan Andrews design

Owner—Bob Lane

Crew—Alan Andrews, Sam Heck, John Jourdane, Keith Ives, Dave Jones,
Bob Greb, Chuck Stevens, Phil Soma, Mat Bryant, Scott Jones, Jared Morford

Bob Lane and *Medicine Man* are fixtures in the Southern California sailing scene. Bob has had several boats named *Medicine Man* (he is a pharmacist), and several have been changed and metamorphosed into updated versions; each time bigger and faster.

Like *Ragtime, Medicine Man* has a special place in my heart. I have sailed in her across the Pacific six times. She is very fast, and easy to sail. The current boat is a 61-foot Alan Andrews design, with water ballast. It is pretty much Alan's Whitbread 60 design, but with a tiller instead of steering wheels.

Bob Lane is a different kind of owner. He loves to work on the boat, and you can often find him sitting on the deck with a lap full of winch parts, or down below tearing apart a clogged toilet. He is not afraid to get his hands dirty.

Medicine Man starting the Newport to Ensenada Race.

Newport Beach to Cabo Race 2005

The races from Southern California to Cabo San Lucas are usually pleasant, warm downwind runs, but once in a while all hell can break loose. That was the case in June, 2005.

Shortly after the start, the legendary Bill Lee 68, *Merlin*, broke its mast, and motored back in to Newport Beach. A couple hours later, the Andrews 70, *Alchemy*, had a rudder problem that caused the lower bearing to come loose, and break the hull near the stern. It was towed into San Diego by the Coast Guard. The Dubois 90, *Genuine Risk*, pulled out and motored into San Diego with damaged canting keel gear. Then, the next day the Trip 50, *Falcon*, broke its steering and was towed into Turtle Bay by the Mexican Navy.

Medicine Man racing to Cabo San Lucas, Mexico

On *Medicine Man*, we were having our own problems. Our Brookes & Gatehouse instruments suddenly went black the first night of the race. We thought the main processor had fried (It turned out a junction box we didn't even know about, under a bunk, was under water). So, we had to sail the rest of the race the old fashion way, with only the compass. We did have the GPS to give us position, course, and speed. But, with no wind direction, it was hard deciding on when to jibe, with no wind speed, it was hard to know when to change sails.

Alan Andrews was steering the boat when we hit a large sunfish, while doing about eighteen knots of boat speed. The sunfish wrapped around the rudder, and Alan couldn't steer. The boat broached, and we were knocked flat with the mast in the water and the rudder out of the water with a sunfish stuck on it. We tried lowering the spinnaker, but the halyard was in its lock and so loaded, we couldn't unlock it. The sails were flailing badly, and I thought we were going to break the mast.

Keith Ives took the initiative, and ran below to get the boat hook. He went to the transom, and poked at the sunfish until it slid off the rudder. Alan did a great job of getting the boat back upright and under control, and we took off again at eighteen to twenty knots of boat speed. Nothing broke and no on was hurt during the incident, except the poor sunfish.

It was a wild night, but we survived without breaking anything, and had a great spinnaker ride past Punta Abreojos to Magdelena Bay. The sun came out, the temperature rose, and we were surfing down nice waves in shorts and T-shirts.

It was a very fast race. We finished the 820-mile race in less than three days. The Andrews 80, *Magnitude*, was first to finish, in two days, thirteen hours. She broke the eighteen-year old record held by *Blondie*. We were happy with our fourth place finish behind the Reichel/Pugh 75, *Scout Spirit*, and the new Dencho 70, *Peligroso*. And after a few margaritas in the hot sun in Cabo, the story about the sunfish wrapped around our rudder got better and better.

Twenty-Three

Broken Rudders and Masts

I've learned a lot about broken gear over the years. Maybe the reader can learn from my mistakes.

My first broken rudder was on a Cal 1/4-tonner in Honolulu. I was helping the Cal dealer show the boat to a potential client. We were sailing off Diamond Head, and the rudder just snapped in two. It was more than a bit embarrassing for the dealer. We hailed a passing fishing boat, which gave us a tow into the harbor.

The next broken rudder was on *Brooke Ann*, sailing from St. Thomas to Ft. Lauderdale after Antigua Race Week. That one was covered earlier in the book. We built the 49-foot *Brooke Ann*, and broke her new carbon fiber rudder in the first race of SORC. Mark Soverel generously lent us a rudder off one of his boats to complete the series.

We trucked *Brooke Ann* back to California from Florida, and built a new rudder, which we actually took to a commercial testing laboratory, and had the shaft tested for strength. I then sailed the boat to Hawaii for the Kenwood Cup. The new rudder broke the day before the first race while we practicing off Honolulu. The crew stayed up all night building a new rudder, which wasn't fast but allowed the boat to finish the series.

Racing across the Atlantic in the Route of Discovery Race on the Santa Cruz 70, *Pyewacket*, we broke our new, light weight carbon rudder, and then broke our emergency rudder. We managed to sail into Turks and Caicos Islands with the eighteen inches of original rudder.

Using a spinnaker pole as a sweep on Brooke Ann.

While racing from San Francisco to Kaneohe Bay in the Pacific Cup, on the fifty-foot *M-Project*, we lost the rudder. It was a brand new carbon rudder that hadn't cured long enough, and the frame holding the blade to the rudder post came unglued. We still had the rudder, but it was spinning on the rudder post. We attached the large plywood/fiberglass emergency rudder, on gudgeons and pintels on the transom, and it snapped within a few minutes. We motor-sailed back to California using a spinnaker pole sweep to steer.

The lessons I learned from all these rudder losses is:

1. Don't go offshore with an untried and untested rudder.
2. Have a real emergency rudder that is deep, very strong and firmly attached to the boat.
3. If you have to use the emergency rudder, don't continue to race; reduce sail, and get to port slowly and safely.

Broken Masts

I have the unenvious distinction of breaking a mast in every ocean on Earth. Granted, I was sailing on race boats pushing the limit, both in construction and trying to sail as fast as possible.

Ondine's mast broke north of Bermuda while bringing the boat back from Europe. We motored to the island of St. Pierre near Newfoundland, got fuel, and motored to Sturgeon Bay, Wisconsin.

Fisher & Paykel's mizzen mast broke in the South Atlantic, near Rio de Janeiro. We finished the leg as a sloop.

Blondie's mast broke about 100 miles out of Honolulu on the delivery back to Long Beach after Transpac. We returned to Honolulu, loaded on fuel, and then motored the boat to Los Angeles.

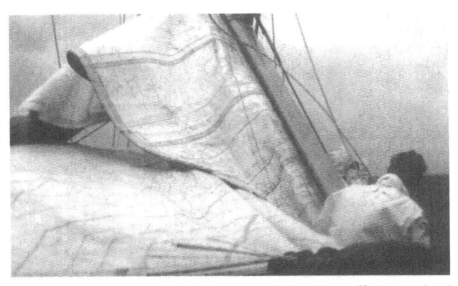

The Farr 40, *Margaret*, broke her mast while sailing off New Zealand. We were able to motor into Auckland Harbor.

We broke *NZI Enterprise's* upper shroud and bent the mast in the Indian Ocean near Cape Town. We shored it up enough to finish the leg into Cape Town.

Then *NZI Enterprise* lost her complete mast in the Southern Ocean between New Zealand and Cape Horn. We jury-rigged a mast, and sailed back to the Chatham Islands off South Island New Zealand.

The lessons I learned from all these broken masts:

1. Pull the mast out regularly, and check for any problems.
2. If you do break a mast, save all the pieces you can to use for your jury rig.
3. If you do have to deep six the rig, have a sledge hammer and drift pin to punch out the clevis pins.
4. Have and extensive set of tools and repair materials to fix any damage that may occur.
5. Be creative in erecting a jury mast and sails.
6. Carry plenty of fuel, because you don't know when you won't have a mast to sail with.

    Be creative

Postscript

There are some true scoundrels out there, and I mean it in the worst sense. They are the polluters and commercial fishermen who don't care about the ocean.

Every time I have crossed the ocean over the past several decades, I have seen more and more trash and oil slicks. I know most of it is from big ships that use the ocean as their dumping grounds, not the recreational boater.

I also see more and more big commercial fishing ships (both long-liners and net boats). They are emptying the ocean of fish to make a buck; indiscriminately catching all sea life, and then only keeping the commercially valuable species.

I know most of them are foreign fishing and cruise ships in international waters, and there isn't much we can do to stop them. But we have to try to do something, before the ocean is a toxic, lifeless dump.

We can each do our part by not throwing any trash or pollutants overboard, and also by supporting any antipollution and anticommercial fishing organizations that are standing up to the unethical commercial interests.

Glossary

ABAFT	farther toward the stern; the mizzenmast is abaft the mainmast.
ABEAM	at right angles to the centerline of the boat, but not on the boat.
ABOARD	on or in the boat.
ADRIFT	loose from its moorings; not made fast to any stationary object.
AFT	near or toward the stern of the boat.
AGROUND	touching or stuck on the bottom.
AHEAD	in the direction of, and forward of the bow.
AHOY	term used for hailing a boat.
ALEE	away from the direction of the wind, usually referring to the movement of the helm or tiller.
ALOFT	above the deck, usually in the rigging.
AMIDSHIPS	center portion of a vessel between bow and stern, or between port and starboard sides.
ANCHORAGE	a place suitable for anchoring: usually out of traffic, sheltered, with good holding ground.
ASTERN	in the direction of, and beyond the stern; opposite of ahead.
ATHWARTSHIPS	at right angles to the centerline of a boat.
AUXILIARY	the small engine of a sailing vessel.
BACK	the wind is said to back when it changes its direction counter-clockwise.
BACKSTAY	standing rigging that supports the mast from aft; standing backstay runs from the masthead to the transom. Running backstays run from a point on the mast to a point on the quarter, where they are

	adjusted by winches.
BACKWIND	wind deflected off a boat's sail into the leeward side of another sail; one sail is said to backwind another.
BAR	A shallow entrance to a harbor where waves break dangerously on an ebb tide.
BARE POLES	a sailboat that is underway with no sail set; usually a heavy weather precaution "the yacht bore off before the storm under bare poles."
BARGE	a cargo-carrying vessel, usually without an engine. Also a term in sail racing, a boat forces its way illegally between another contestant and the starting line is said to be barging.
BATTEN DOWN	originally, to secure hatches with canvas covers, held in place by battens; hence, to prepare for a storm.
BEAM	the side or greatest width of a vessel.
BEAM REACH	sailing with the wind at right angles to the boat.
BEAR	to bear down is to approach from windward, to bear off is to sail away to leeward.
BEARING	the direction of an object, expressed as a true bearing or as a relative bearing; relative to some second object, usually one's own vessel.
BEAT	to sail to windward in a series of tacks. Beating is one of the three points of sailing, also known as close-hauled.
BEAUFORT SCALE	a system of describing wind forces by numbers, from 0 for a flat calm to 12 for a hurricane.
BEFORE THE WIND	in the same direction the wind blows, as a point of sailing.
BELAY	to make fast a line to a cleat; also to rescind an order which is being carried out.
BEND	a knot that fastens one line to another; also to attach a sail to a mast or rigging.
BERTH	a sailor's bed; also a vessel's allotted place at a pier or marina.
BILGE	the interior of the hull below the floorboards.
BINNACLE	a stand containing the steering compass.

BITTER END	the last part of a rope or final link of chain.
BLANKET	a sail that is deprived of wind by an intervening sail or boat is said to be blanketed.
BLOCK	nautical word for pulley; two or more blocks with a rope through them form a tackle.
BLOOPER	A sail shaped like half a spinnaker that is carried with the spinnaker to help balance the boat.
BOARD	one tack of a series; often an uneven series of long boards and short boards.
BOLT ROPE	line stitched to the foot and luff of a sail to give it strength or the substitute for sail slides.
BOOM	spar to which the foot of a sail is attached, and which itself is attached to the mast.
BOOM VANG	a tackle running between the boom and deck which flattens the sail's curve by downward pull on the boom.
BOSUN'S CHAIR	(Boatswain's Chair)plank seat made fast to a halyard, for a man to sit on while working aloft.
BOSUN'S SLING	same as a bosun's chair, but uses a climbing harness instead of a plank.
BOW	the forward part of a vessel.
BOWLINE	knot used to form a temporary eye or loop in the end of a line.
BOWSPRIT	a spar extending forward of the bow and set into the deck, to support headsails.
BRIGHTWORK	polished metal fittings or varnished woodwork.
BROACH	a boat broaches when, while running free, it swings out of control and beam-on to the wind.
BROAD REACH	sailing with wind more or less over either quarter.
BULKHEAD	a vertical partition separating parts of the boat.
BY THE LEE	running with the wind on the same side as the main boom; dangerous, because it invites an accidental jibe.
BUNK	a sailor's bed.
CABIN	the enclosed or decked-over living space of a boat.
CAPSIZE	to turn over.
CARRY AWAY	to break free.

CAST OFF	to let go, to let a line go.
CATAMARAN	a boat with two hulls joined at the center.
CENTERBOARD	a plate or board that can be raised or lowered through a slot in the bottom of a boat.
CENTER OF EFFORT	the center of wind pressure on a sail.
CHAFE	to wear a sail, spar, or line by rubbing it again something. This is prevented by using chafing gear.
CHAIN PLATE	metal strap bolted or fiber glassed to the side of a sailboat, to which a shroud or stay is attached.
CHEEK BLOCK	a block whose sheave is mounted against a spar.
CHINE	the line formed by the intersection of the side and bottom of a flat or V-bottomed boat.
CHOCK	a U-shaped fairlead secured in or on a boat's rail, for anchor and mooring lines.
CLEAT	a horned fitting of wood or metal to which lines are made fast.
CLEW	the lower after corner of a sail.
CLOSE-HAULED	Sailing as close as possible to the wind.
CLOSE REACH	sailing with sheets eased and the wind forward of the beam.
COCKPIT	the well in a boat's deck from which the crew handles her operation.
COIL	to lay a line down in circular turns.
COURSE	the direction steered by a vessel.
CORDAGE	a general term for all types of rope.
CRADLE	a wooden framework supporting a boat out of the water.
CRINGLE	a ring sewn into a sail through which a line can pass.
CRUISING REACHER	a high-cut jib sail used for cruising.
CURRENT	the horizontal movement of water, caused by a tide or wind, or both.
DAGGER BOARD	a type of center board that does not pivot, but is raised and lowered vertically.

DINGHY	a small boat, usually designed to be carried as a tender to a larger boat. May be rigged for sail.
DISPLACEMENT	the weight of water displaced by a floating vessel; hence the weight of the vessel itself.
DITTY BAG	a small bag for a sailor's sewing kit and other tools relating to sails and rope.
DOUSE	to lower a sail quickly.
DOWNHAUL	tackle attached to the underside of the gooseneck, to tighten a sail's luff by pulling down on the boom.
DOWNWIND	to leeward, away from the wind.
DRAFT	the depth of water to the lowest point of the vessel's keel.
EASE	to slacken.
EASTING	Getting east – important when sailing into the trade winds from west to east.
EVEN KEEL	a boat is on an even keel when it is floating level.
EYE OF THE WIND	the direction from which the wind is coming.
EYE SPLICE	a permanent loop in the end of a rope.
FALL OFF	to let a boat's head turn away from the wind.
FAST	secure; to make something fast is to secure it.
FENDER	a portable ant chafing device, usually tubular, placed between a boat and a pier or another boat.
FLAKE	a full turn in a coil of rope; a method of laying out rope in figure-eights, to run freely; method of placing a sail in layers across a spar.
FLAT SEAS	waves less than one foot high.
FOOT	the lower edge of a sail.
FORE AND AFT	in line with the keel.
FOREPEAK	a compartment in the very bow.
FORESTAY	a stay below and aft of the jibstay on a yacht carrying two headsails.
FORWARD	toward the bow.
FOULED	jammed or entangled; not clear. Said of any piece of equipment.
FREEBOARD	the vertical distance from the waterline to the

	gunwale.
FLUKE	the palm of an anchor.
FULL AND BY	close-hauled.
GASKET	a sail stop.
GHOST	a sailboat moving in little or no wind is said to be ghosting.
GO ABOUT	same as come about.
GOOSENECK	the moveable fitting connecting mast and boom.
GROUND TACKLE	collective term for anchor and associated gear: cable, chain, swivel, and so forth.
GUNWHALE	pronounced gunnel, the upper edge of a boat's side.
HALYARD	line or wire used for hoisting sails.
HARD ALEE	the command given to put the boat about, by pushing the tiller to leeward.
HEADSAILS	sails forward of the foremost mast; includes jibs, genoas, spinnakers, and spinnaker staysails.
HEAD UP	to head into the wind.
HEADWAY	boat's forward momentum.
HEAD	the upper corner of a triangular sail; also the toilet.
HEEL	to tip to one side.
HELM	the tiller or wheel. The man steering is the helmsman.
HITCH	properly, a method of making a rope fast to another rope or to a spar.
IN IRONS	stuck midway through coming about.
JIB	triangular sail set ahead of the foremost sail.
JIB SHEET	line controlling the jib.
JIB STAY	stay running from bow to the mast, on which the jib is set. If the stay runs to the masthead, it may be called a headstay.
JIBE	to bring the wind to the opposite side of the boat when sailing with the wind aft by turning the stern across the wind.
JUMPER	stay on the upper forward part of the mast.
KEEL	the weighted, deepest part of the hull, used to give

	the boat stability and prevent capsize.
KEEL BOAT	a boat with a fixed keel, as opposed to a center-board boat.
KETCH	a two-masted sailboat in which the smaller after-mast, the mizzen, is stepped forward of the rudder post.
KNOCKDOWN	said of a boat that is laid over suddenly, by wind or sea, so that water pours over the gunwale.
KNOT	a speed of one nautical mile (6080 feet) per hour. A knot is not a measure of distance, but a rate of speed.
LANYARD	a short line, usually attached to some piece of loose gear, for making it fast.
LAY	to lay a mark is to be able to reach it in a single tack, close-hauled. The lay of a line is the direction in which its strands are twisted.
LAZARETTE	compartment for gear stowage at the stern of the boat.
LEECH	the after edge of a fore-and-aft sail.
LEE HELM	a boat out of balance, so as to turn away from the wind when the helm is amidships, is said to carry lee helm.
LEEWARD	pronounced loo-ard, the direction away from the wind.
LIGHT SAILS	sails make of extra-light material, such as the spinnaker and drifter.
LOCKER	a stowage compartment.
LONG SPLICE	a method of permanently joining the ends of two ropes without increasing the diameter.
LOOSE-FOOTED	said of a sail that secures to the boom at tack and clew only.
LUFF	the forward edge of a sail; also to head up into the wind, thus causing the sail to ripple.
MAHIMAHI	(or MAHI) Hawaiian name for dolphin fish (not the mammal dolphin) also called Dorado.
MAINMAST	the principal mast of a boat.
MAINSAIL	the sail that sets abaft the mainmast.

MAINSHEET	the sheet controlling the mainsail.
MIZZEN	the after and smaller mast of a ketch or yawl. Also the sail set on that mast.
MOORING	large anchor permanently in place, to which is attached a line or chain with a buoy at the top.
OFF THE WIND	sailing on a reach or run.
OUTBOARD	toward or beyond the boat's side.
OUTHAUL	device for stretching the foot of a sail along the boom.
PAINTER	dinghy tow rope or dockline.
PINCH	to sail a boat closer to the wind than she can efficiently go.
POINT	ability to sail close to the wind.
PORT	the left side of a vessel, looking forward.
PORT TACK	sailing with the wind coming over a boat's port side.
PREVENTER	a guy line led forward from the end of a boom or pole to keep it from accidentally swinging.
PUFF	a gust of wind.
QUARTER	the part of a boat lying with forty-five degrees of the stern; every boat has a port and starboard quarter.
RAKE	the angle of a vessel's mast from the perpendicular.
REACH	the point of sailing between close-hauled and running.
READY ABOUT	preparatory order given before, "Hard alee," to put the boat about.
REEF	to reduce the area of sail.
REEF POINTS	short lines put into the sail to aid in reefing.
RIGGING	general term for the lines (wire and rope) that control the hoisting and set of the sails (running rigging).
ROACH	the curve in the leech of a sail.
RODE	anchor line.
RUDDER	a steering device at the stern of a boat.
RUNNING	sailing with the wind astern.

RUNNING RIGGING	sheets, halyards, topping lifts, outhauls.
SEA ROOM	safe distance from the shore or other hazards.
SEAWORTHY	said of a boat or boat's gear in fit condition to meet the sea.
SECURE	to make fast.
SEIZE	to bind with a thin line.
SHACKLE	a U-shaped connector with a removable pin.
SHEAVE	the grooved wheel in a block.
SHEET	the line used to trim a sail.
SHEET BEND	a knot used to join two ropes.
SHROUD	standing rigging that supports a mast athwart ships.
SLACK	not fastened; loose. Also to loosen.
SLOOP	a sailboat with a single mast whose working sails are a main and jib.
SNATCH BLOCK	a block that opens at the side, so a bight of line can be inserted or removed without reeving the entire line through it.
SPARS	general term for masts, boom, gaffs, which have in common that they hold sails extended.
SPINNAKER	a headsail used in running and reaching.
SPLICE	to permanently join two lines by tucking their strands alternately over and under each other.
SQUALL	sudden, violent gust of wind, often accompanied by rain.
STANDING PART	the part of a rope that is made fast.
STANDING RIGGING	shrouds and stays supporting the mast.
STARBOARD	the right side of a vessel, facing forward.
STARBOARD TACK	sailing with the wind coming over a boat's starboard side.
STAY	rigging supporting the mast from forward or aft.
STAYSAIL	name for several types of sail having the luff secured to a stay.
STEERAGEWAY	enough motion for the rudder to be effective.
STEM	the bow of the boat.

STERN	the after part of the boat.
STOP	strap, piece of line, or length of shock cord used to lash a furled sail.
STORM JIB	a very small jib set in heavy weather.
STOW	to put in place.
SWAMP	to fill a boat with water.
TACK	to come about; the lower forward corner of a sail; to sail on port or starboard tack.
TACKLE	a purchase made up of blocks and line.
TELLTALE	a wind direction indicator made of a bit of yarn or other light material tied to a shroud.
THWARTS	seats in a boat.
TILLER	the lever with which the rudder is turned.
TOPPING LIFT	adjustable line from the masthead supporting the boom.
TRAVELER	an athwarships track or bar on which the main-sheet is led.
TURNBUCKLE	a tensioning device used with shrouds and stays.
UNDER WAY	said of a boat in motion and under control.
WAKE	a vessel's visible track through the water.
WAY ON	moving through the water, a boat is said to have way on.
WEATHER	the windward side of the boat.
WEATHER HELM	opposite of lee helm; the tendency of a boat with its rudder amidships to turn by itself to windward.
WHIPPING	method of keeping a rope's end from unlaying.
WINDEX	a masthead vane to see wind direction.
WIND'S EYE	the exact direction from which the wind is coming.
WINDWARD	the general direction from which the wind is coming.
WING	(AND-Wing) sailing with the mainsail eased out and a jib sail poled out on the opposite side of the boat. Only works while running dead downwind.
YAWL	a two-masted vessel whose small mizzen is stepped abaft the rudder post.

About the Author

John Jourdane was born and raised in Southern California. He received his Bachelor's degree in Zoology from UCLA and a Master's degree in Education at USC. After a two-year stint in the Peace Corps in Colombia, he taught science in Hawaii for ten years. Then he left teaching and went sailing. He has spent the last thirty years racing, delivering, and cruising the oceans of the world.

John has sailed over 300,000 miles including forty-seven Pacific crossings, twelve Atlantic crossings, and in virtually every offshore race in the world including two Whitbread Round the World Races. He has appeared on television and radio talking about yacht racing.

He is the author of the book, *Icebergs, Port and Starboard,* and is considered one of the most experienced and respected offshore yachtsmen in the world.